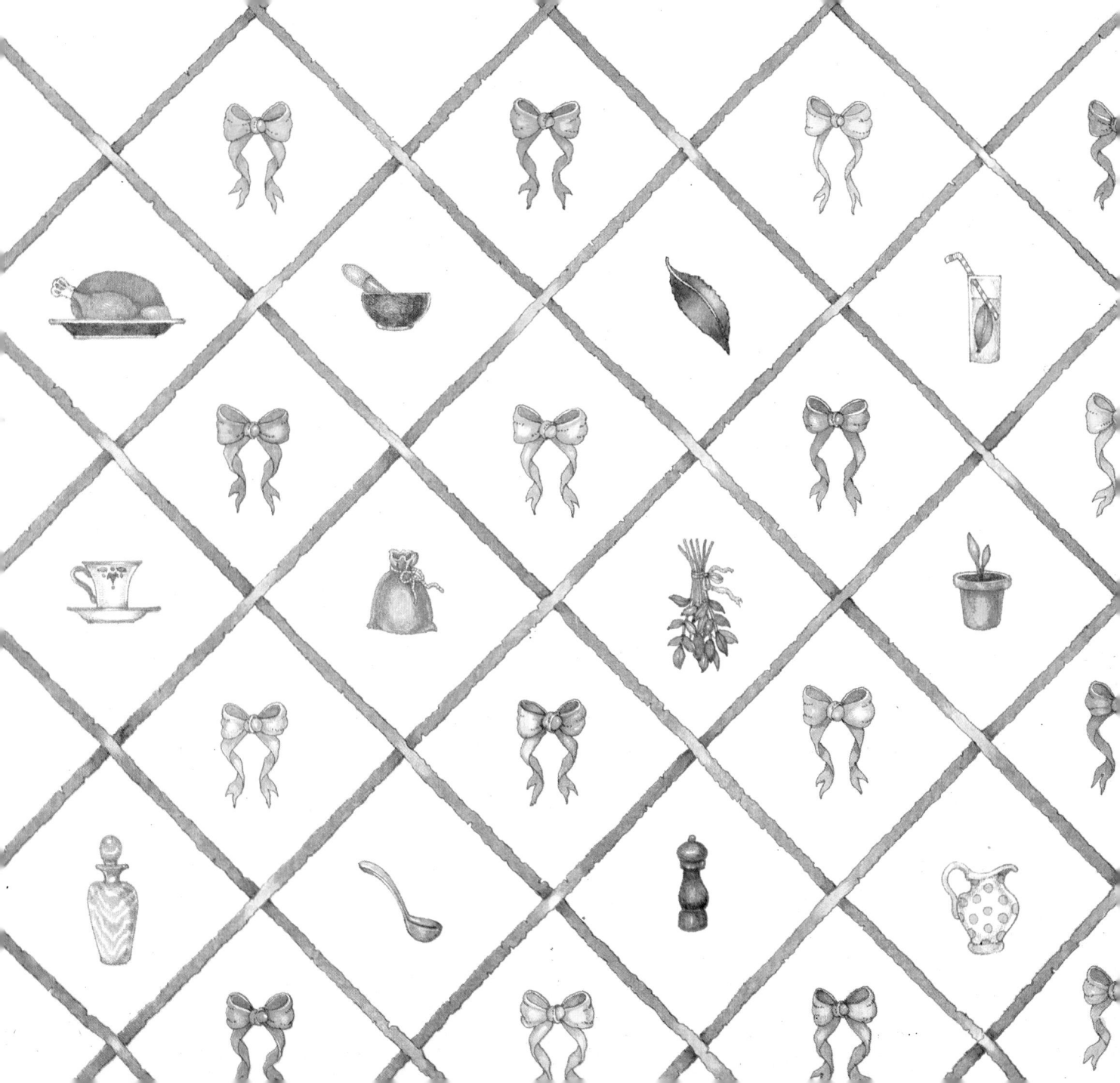

A BOOK OF

HERBS
&
SPICES

A BOOK OF
HERBS
&
SPICES

Recipes, Remedies and Lore

•

GAIL DUFF
ILLUSTRATED BY CHERRY DENMAN

MEREHURST PRESS
LONDON

Published 1987 by
Merehurst Press
Ferry House, 51-57 Lacy Road,
Putney, London SW15 1PR
By arrangement with Breslich & Foss

Reprinted 1989

Designed and produced by
Breslich & Foss
Golden House
28-31 Great Pulteney Street
London W1R 3DD

Editor: Judy Martin
Editorial assistant: Jim Abram
Designer: Roger Daniels
Paste-up artist: Elly King

ISBN 0-948075-74-0 CASED
ISBN 1-85391-118-6 LIMP

Typeset by AKM Associates (UK) Ltd, London.
Printed and bound in Spain by Sirven Grafic, Barcelona.

Contents

Cultivation and Use

There is nothing new in the use of herbs and spices. They have enriched human life for thousands of years, providing both comfort and luxury. They have flavoured our food, cured our ailments and surrounded us with sweet scents. They have also played a part in our folklore and magic. It would be a very different world without them.

No one really knows who first used herbs and spices, or for what purpose. All their properties were known to the ancient Greeks and Egyptians and to those living in early Biblical times. The knowledge that they employed, and that we still use today, must have been based on the trial and error of early man who was originally drawn to the plants because of their tantalizing aroma. He gradually discovered their individual effects on his food and his well-being; crudely, no doubt, but we are still basing our use of aromatic plants on those early experiments.

Herbs and spices are generally spoken of together since they are used for similar purposes. The basic difference between them is that what we call 'herbs' are typically the foliage of a plant, used either fresh or dried, and 'spices' are mainly the dried fruits. There are, however, other differences that have influenced their history more.

Herbs are the more humble of the two. Most were first discovered in Europe, around the Mediterranean or in Asia, and since their discovery have been transplanted to many countries of the world. They are small plants which are easily manageable and best suited to being grown in private gardens rather than in plantations. Many are hardy, despite coming from warm climates, and quite able to withstand the colder winters of temperate regions. As a result, most people have always had access to herbs of some kind. They were gathered at first, then transplanted to the neighbourhood of rough settlements, and later grown in more formal gardens. No one has fought over supplies of herbs, there have been few great expeditions to find them and nobody has either been ruined or made a fortune by them. They have always been homely plants, available when needed.

'the friend of physicians and the praise of cooks'
CHARLEMAGNE

Most spices, on the other hand, come from exotic, tropical climes and were originally carried on long and perilous journeys to make them available to the Western world. In early times their origins were jealously guarded and many were the tales of venomous beasts or ferocious birds dreamed up by merchants to deter others from encroaching on the sources of their spice monopoly. In these times, demand for spices was always greater than the supplies. They were expensive and available only to the rich and privileged. As early as the thirteenth century, Europeans set out on treacherous sea voyages, determined to find the Spice Islands and win fame and riches for both themselves and their countries. Many men died in the quest for spices, countries were won and lost, ships sunk and fortunes made. We may now treat them as cheap, everyday commodities, but this has not always been so.

For centuries herbs and spices were appreciated to the full, but in modern times the shortages caused by world wars and then the arrival of the convenience foods and patent medicines of the twentieth century almost made us forget them. But anything that has been so much loved and valued can never be completely neglected and, thanks to a few dedicated cooks and herbalists, the knowledge was kept alive. The wheel is now coming full circle. In our present day quest for all things natural, herbs and spices have come into their own again. While we are rediscovering their endless uses in the kitchen and around the home, it is intriguing to learn of their fascinating histories and lore and to experience the pleasures of tending a herb garden.

Growing Herbs

Growing herbs, whether on a large or small scale, is an absolute pleasure and not at all difficult. Herbs are extremely tolerant plants and although each one favours its own particular growing conditions and soil type, most will thrive together in a warm, sheltered corner of the garden.

— THE HERB PLOT —

Your outdoor herb plot can be large or small, depending on the space you have available and the number of different herbs that you wish to grow. Ideally it should be sheltered and open to the sun for most of the day, with a partially shaded area at one end for those herbs that do not like full sun; if this is not possible, choose the warmest spot available.

The shape and arrangement of your herb garden is again subject to personal taste and the size and shape of your plot. You may prefer a wide border down one side of a lawn or patio, or a central bed. If you would like to make the herbs a special feature of your garden, you will need only a little extra time to lay them out in the fashion of an Elizabethan knot garden. You can save time on weeding by planting them in a chequerboard pattern of paving stones, making small, square, easily cared for beds. A small, circular plot can be arranged cartwheel fashion by marking it out with small stones in eight divisions from a central 'hub'. Herbs can also be grown among vegetables or in flower beds and borders.

Keep the herb garden well weeded and water it regularly during dry summer weather. If possible, give it a dressing of well-rotted farmyard manure or compost every autumn.

— PREPARATION AND PLANTING —

Before planting any herbs, dig in some well-rotted farmyard manure or compost and if the soil is on the acid side, add a little lime. When it comes to planting out the herbs, think about how they are going to look when they have grown to full height and are in flower. Arrange them so that the taller ones will not hide the smaller ones from view or shade them from the sun, and also so that they will look attractive when growing together.

— PERENNIAL HERBS —

Perennial plants can be bedded out in either spring or autumn. After flowering, they should all be cut back to prevent them from becoming straggly. Some, such as thyme, marjoram and savory, remain usable during the winter, although their stems are shorter and their leaves tougher and smaller. Rosemary leaves also become slightly tougher but they remain just as prolific. Other perennials, such as fennel or chives, disappear completely after the first frosts and will begin to grow again in early spring. Most perennials can be propagated by root division and old plants should be replaced at least every four years. Do not dig up the old plants until the new ones have become completely established.

— ANNUAL HERBS —

Annual herbs are usually sown in spring and some can be sown at regular intervals throughout the summer to ensure successive cropping. Some are best sown directly into their growing positions — dill, for example. Others, such as basil, are best started off in trays or pots under glass or on a sunny windowsill. You can rely on some annuals — angelica is one — to seed themselves, but others must be resown each year.

— TUBS AND WINDOW BOXES —

If you have only a small garden, or perhaps none at all, you can still grow herbs. Tubs or large terracotta pots make an attractive feature on patios and balconies. Wooden barrels, cut in half and treated with a wood preservative, can also be used. Mount them on bricks and fill them when they are in position; they will be too heavy to carry otherwise. Put stones or broken crockery in the bottom of the containers, then half-fill them with a mixture of soil and shingle and finally top with a good growing medium.

Window boxes should be filled in a similar way, but insert a layer of wire mesh before you put in the stones or crocks.

Herbs in tubs and window boxes should be kept small and bushy by regular cutting back.

— HERBS IN POTS AND BASKETS —

The smaller culinary herbs can be grown in pots indoors. Parsley, chives, thyme, sage, marjoram, rosemary and basil are the most suitable. The pots should be 6–8 inches (15–20cm) in diameter. Put stones or broken crockery in the bottom and fill them with a standard potting medium or with a mixture of garden compost and soil with a little coarse sand. Indoor herbs need plenty of light, warmth during the day and a cooler temperature at night. Water them regularly but do not over-water.

A delightful way of growing fresh herbs around the house is to place them in hanging baskets. Pressed paper moulds and sphagnum moss for lining the baskets can be bought at garden centres.

So universal was this dependence on native products, that in cottage garden or castle plaisance there was always a bed of herbs, or a nook set aside for their culture.

MARTHA B. FLINT
A Garden of Simples,
1900

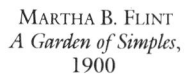

Preserving Herbs

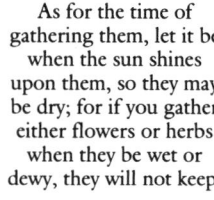

Most herbs will produce more leaves than it is possible to use in one summer, but do not let them go to waste. Preserve them for the winter either by drying or by freezing.

— HARVESTING —

Herbs can be gathered for preserving from midsummer until autumn. Shrubby perennial herbs, such as thyme, marjoram and savory, and also some annuals should ideally be cut just before the flower buds open as it is then that their scent and flavour are strongest.

Choose a dry, sunny day and cut after the dew has dried but before the sun is at its strongest. Use strong, sharp scissors so as not to damage the plants. You can safely harvest about one-third of the perennial herbs, but do not do so indiscriminately. Try to shape the plant at the same time so

that it will grow evenly bushy. Annual herbs, such as sweet basil, summer savory and dill can be cut 3–4 inches (7.5–10cm) from the ground. Cutting the central spikes will encourage the side shoots to grow thickly.

Unless you are pruning and tidying at the same time, pick only as many herbs as you can deal with in one day. Discard any blemished or discoloured sprigs and handle the leaves as little as possible. Take the herbs indoors immediately after cutting.

— DRYING HERBS —

Small quantities of seeds for home use can be simply tied in small bunches using fine cotton string. Hang them in a warm, dry, airy place, away from direct sunlight. A warm spare room is ideal, or a dry, warm closet. In a centrally heated space of any size, the temperature should not exceed 90°F (30°C).

Drying racks for single leaves and flowers can be improvised by spreading butter muslin over cake-cooling racks. You can purpose-build drying racks quite simply by constructing oblong frames of light wood, each one strengthened with a diagonal cross piece, and stretching hessian or butter muslin over them. When stacked they should allow a good flow of air between the racks. Like the bunches of herbs, racks should be kept in a warm, dry, airy room.

The herbs dry out within four to

As for the time of gathering them, let it be when the sun shines upon them, so they may be dry; for if you gather either flowers or herbs when they be wet or dewy, they will not keep.

NICHOLAS CULPEPER, 1640

five days. They should have maintained a bright, fresh colour and both twigs and leaves should snap crisply. If they are not completely dry, they may reabsorb moisture during storage and become musty.

To preserve the flavour of the leaves and flowers, strip them carefully from the stems, leaving them whole. They can be crushed when needed.

When harvesting seeds, pick whole flowerheads together with about 6 inches (15cm) of stalk when the seeds are full but not quite brown. Place brown paper bags over the seedheads and hang them upside down. After about five days the seeds will have dropped into the bags.

Dried herbs and seeds are best kept in jars or tins that are both air-tight and light-proof. If only see-through jars are available, cover them with a self-adhesive covering.

Dried herbs will keep for six to eight months. Any left can be added to the compost heap, scattered on the herb garden or sprinkled around pot plants. If you have an open fire, a handful of dried herbs scattered over the flames pleasantly perfumes the room.

— FREEZING HERBS —

The best herbs for freezing are those with large, fleshy leaves, such as basil, mint and parsley, and those with a delicate texture such as fennel and dill.

There is no need to blanch herbs before freezing. Put whole leaves, in usable amounts, inside small polythene bags or wrap them in plastic clingfilm. Freeze these separately and then pack them into labelled boxes, one for each herb. Ready-tied *bouquets garnis* can be frozen in the same way. Use the herbs straight from the freezer, either adding whole sprigs to a dish to be removed before serving, or chopping them while they are still frozen solid.

Another way to freeze herbs is to chop them first and pack them into ice-cube trays so that each compartment is about two-thirds full. Top them with cold water and freeze them. These frozen herb cubes can be added directly to sauces, soups, sauté dishes and casseroles. You can do this with single herbs or mixtures.

— HERB VINEGARS —

Herb vinegar is an excellent way to preserve the flavour of herbs for use with salads. Steep a sprig of fresh herbs in a bottle of white wine vinegar on a sunny windowsill for three weeks. Change the herb sprig for a fresh one and store the vinegar in the larder or kitchen closet. It can be used immediately but will keep for a year.

Herbs and Spices in the Kitchen

However good our basic ingredients may be, the dishes that we make with them will always be improved by the subtle use of a herb or spice. If you are new to herbs and spices, use them sparingly at first, one at a time or in simple mixtures. When you have learned their flavours and their effects on different foods you can start to experiment.

— BOUQUET GARNI —

The basic *bouquet garni* consists of a sprig each of thyme, parsley and chervil, plus a bay leaf. If you have no chervil, use two parsley sprigs instead. Tie them together with fine cotton string.

Use a *bouquet garni* to flavour stocks, soups, marinades, stews, casseroles and braised dishes. Add it at the beginning of cooking time and remove it before serving. The basic formula can be changed according to your dish. For example, add a rosemary sprig and a piece of lemon thyme for lamb, a sage leaf for pork, or fennel for fish.

— SPICE MIXTURES —

India has its curry powders and garam masala, China a five-spice powder consisting of anise pepper, star anise, cinnamon, cloves and fennel, and in Britain a mixture of sweet spices is used in baking. The main ingredient of pickling spice is mustard seeds and to this can be added chillies, cloves, black peppercorns, coriander seeds or juniper berries.

— WITH MEAT —

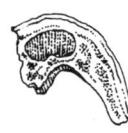

Chopped herbs are generally added to casseroles, stews and braised or sauté dishes as soon as the meat has come to the boil in the liquid. Sprigs of herbs can be placed on roasting or pot-roasting meat or on hot grill racks.

Spices are generally added to meat dishes before the liquid, and benefit from being gently sautéed with onions and garlic. They can be rubbed over poultry and joints of meat before roasting or boiling, or added to an oil baste for grilled meats.

— WITH VEGETABLES —

Add a sprig of herbs to boiling and steaming vegetables or toss plainly cooked vegetables in butter and chop-

ped herbs. Add chopped herbs or a *bouquet garni* to braised vegetables, or to vegetables being simmered in a small amount of water. Sprinkle chopped herbs over grilled vegetables.

— SALADS AND DRESSINGS —

A mixture of chopped fresh green herbs can be added to any green salad to great advantage, and in smaller quantities lend special flavour to creamed and vinaigrette dressings. A pinch of spice can also be added to vinaigrette and to mayonnaise.

— STUFFINGS —

Stuffings for meats, poultry and vegetables such as marrow or courgettes can all contain appropriate mixtures of chopped herbs and small amounts of spices, depending on the character of the recipe and the final flavour required.

— BUTTERS —

Savoury butters are based on unsalted butter. The butter is creamed and flavourings of chopped herbs, crushed garlic and savoury spices such as curry powder and cumin are beaten in. The mixture is formed into a roll, chilled and cut into pats which can be eaten fresh or stored in the freezer.

Beat small amounts of the sweet spices, with some sugar, into unsalted butter and use as a topping for hot fruits and puddings.

— CHEESES AND DIPS —

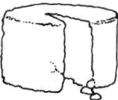

Cream cheese, curd cheese and low-fat soft cheeses can all be flavoured with finely chopped fresh herbs. Spices can be mixed with grated cheese to make toppings for toast and savoury dishes.

A variety of dips can also be made using soft cheese, yoghurt or soured cream flavoured with herb and spice mixtures.

— SAUCES —

Classic sauces such as Béarnaise would not be the same without their flavouring of herbs and a béchamel is much improved if the milk is first infused with peppercorns and mace, or if chopped herbs are added after making. Brown sauces and gravies are delicious when simmered with a *bouquet garni*.

— SALT AND SUGAR —

To make herb salts, mix equal quantities of dried herbs and non-iodised salt. Spread on a baking sheet and put into the oven at lowest heat, with the door ajar, for 30 minutes.

Sugar that has been stored with whole spices or a sprig of herbs such as lemon thyme or sweet cicely, can be sprinkled on desserts or used in making sweet sauces and custards.

— DRINKS —

Whole and ground spices are often used to flavour mulled drinks and punches. Herb teas, or tisanes, are becoming increasingly popular and you can buy them in sachets either singly or mixed, or mix your own. Brew herb teas in the same way as ordinary tea. They may be sweetened with a little honey but do not require milk.

Herbs and Spices as Medicine

Herbs and, to a lesser extent, spices, have been used medicinally for thousands of years and modern research is proving that they still have their place in present day cures.

— GENERAL HEALTH —

Simply adding a wide variety of herbs to your daily menus can help towards good health. Many of them contain vitamins, minerals and trace elements, all of which are essential constituents of a nutritious diet, and some have special properties which aid digestion. Flavouring dishes with clever combinations of herbs and spices will help you to develop a taste for a healthier salt-free diet.

Herbal teas tend to be either calming and soothing or reviving and refreshing, and none contain the caffeine present in ordinary tea and in coffee which can cause sleeplessness or increased heart rate. Tending herbs is in itself a relaxing and pleasurable occupation, and sitting or walking in an aromatic garden also has therapeutic effects.

— MINOR COMPLAINTS —

Many minor everyday complaints such as the common cold or nervous indigestion can be eased considerably with herbal treatments. Scratches, bumps and bruises can be similarly treated. However, if you suspect that you have something other than a minor complaint, go to your general practitioner for a reliable diagnosis. After that you can decide to seek out alternative treatment from a homeopath or qualified medical herbalist.

This book is not intended as a manual of herbal treatments, but it provides guidelines on medicinal uses of the herbs and spices to stimulate interest in past and present application of natural remedies for minor ailments.

— HERBAL REMEDIES —

Fresh or dried herbs used in everyday treatments are generally made into liquid preparations.

An infusion is made like ordinary tea. The chopped fresh or crumbled dried herb is put into a pot and boiling water poured on to it. The pot is then covered and the herb left to brew for 10 minutes. The liquid is strained and drunk hot.

To make a decoction, the chopped fresh or crumbled dried herb is boiled in water for a given period, removed from the heat and left, covered, to brew. It is strained before use.

A maceration consists of sprigs of the fresh or dried herb steeped in alcohol, vinegar or oil, depending on the treatment, for some days. The liquid is strained before use.

Herbs

Alecost

TANASETUM BALSAMETA

Freshly scented, bitter-sweet alecost is so-called because it was once used to give a bitter flavour to ale. Its other name, Costmary, is said to come from the Latin *costus amarus*, a bitter shrub, although the final part of the name was in medieval times associated with the Virgin Mary, to whom it was dedicated. Nicholas Culpeper called it the balsam herb, and in America it acquired the name of Bible Leaf because the large grey-green leaves were found to make excellent bookmarks.

Alecost is a native of Central Asia now naturalized in southern Europe. It was cultivated in Spain for export in the sixteenth century and by the mid seventeenth century had become one of the most common of herbs in English cottage gardens.

— CULTIVATION —

Alecost is a perennial herb which likes to grow in a light soil in full sun. To encourage plenty of leaf growth, remove any dead leaves in spring, cut back the flower stalks as soon as they bloom, and trim the whole plant in the autumn.

After about three years, the plants will become woody and straggly, so divide the roots in spring and replant the divided clumps about 20 inches (50cm) apart. Alecost will not seed itself in a temperate climate.

— CULINARY USES —

When alecost was first grown in Britain the leaves were used as a pot-herb or added to salads. They were also highly regarded for the excellent flavour that they imparted when steeped in ale or beer. In country districts they were used as a substitute for mace in puddings.

In present day dishes, alecost adds a slightly bitter mint-like flavour but must be used sparingly. Add it to stews or casseroles of game, chicken or veal, and to sausages and meat

'. . tyed up with small bundles of lavender topes; these they put in the middle of them to lye upon the toppes of beds, presses, etc. for the sweet scent and savour it casteth.'

JOHN PARKINSON, 1629

loaves. A very small amount can be tossed into a green salad.

— MEDICINAL USES—

An infusion of alecost is mildly antiseptic. Since the sixteenth century, it has been drunk, sweetened with honey, as a cure for catarrh. The same infusion is very soothing when rubbed on bee stings and it has also been considered a remedy for an upset stomach.

An ointment made from the leaves was thought to be good for healing spots and sores. Culpeper recommended that it should be made by boiling the leaves 'with oil of olive, and adder's tongue with it'.

— HOUSEHOLD USES —

A chief use of alecost was as a strewing herb 'to sweeten floors and closets'. It was tied with lavender and placed in beds and in the linen cupboard, used in pot-pourri and to make sweet washing waters for the table. Today the roots are used in the manufacture of expensive perfumes.

Alecost Ale

1 gallon (UK), 1¼ gallons (US) (4.5 litres) water
8 oz (225g) alecost leaves
thinly pared rind and juice of a lemon
1 lb (450g) demerara or coarse sugar
1 oz (25g) cream of tartar
1 tablespoon dried brewers' yeast
4 teaspoons demerara or coarse sugar for bottling

Bring the water to the boil. Add the alecost leaves and lemon rind and boil for 10 minutes.

Put the sugar and cream of tartar into a large container, such as a plastic bucket. Strain in the liquid from the alecost leaves. Stir until the sugar dissolves. Allow to cool to blood heat. Add the lemon juice and sprinkle in the yeast. Cover the container. Leave the liquid to ferment in a warm place for 3 days, or until fermentation stops.

Rack the liquid into bottles, adding ½ teaspoon demerara sugar per 1 pint (575ml). Leave the bottles until the ale is clear, about one week.

Angelica

ANGELICA OFFICINALIS

Angelica is a very lush plant. It has thick, hollow stems, large, bright green leaves and a deliciously pungent sweet scent. It is one of the few herbs that flourishes in a cool damp climate and the wild variety grows in profusion in Scandinavia and northern Europe, Scotland and southern England, and in northern regions of the USA.

Europeans of the Anglo-Saxon period knew angelica well. It was not introduced to Britain until the middle of the sixteenth century, but it soon became a common garden plant used medicinally and in the kitchen and the still-room, in both country and town.

— CULTIVATION —

Angelica is a biennial plant that likes partial shade and a rich but not too heavy soil, kept well watered during dry weather. Sow the seeds in early autumn, 1 inch (2.5cm) deep in drills. Plant them out 6 inches (12.5cm) apart the following spring and 2 feet (60cm) or move apart at the end of the first summer.

If you are growing the plant specifically for the leaves and stems, cut off the flowering heads as soon as they appear in early summer. If you do not, the leaves will soon turn yellow. However, if one flowering head is left on the plant, angelica will readily seed itself, rendering further sowings unnecessary. Cut back all the stems of the old plants in late summer.

— CULINARY USES —

For many centuries, the stems and roots of angelica have been candied to be used as sweetmeats and as decoration for sweet dishes. Stalks and leaves add a pungent sweetness when cooked with tart fruits, whether for cold desserts, pies or jams. Both vermouth and Chartreuse owe their distinctive flavours to angelica and it is combined with juniper to make gin.

In Lapland, Norway, Iceland and Siberia, the midribs of angelica leaves are cooked and eaten like asparagus and the dried ground roots are added to rye bread. Angelica leaves can also be used to flavour soups and stews and are very good with white fish.

— MEDICINAL USES —

There is a story that the archangel Michael appeared to a monk in a dream and informed him that angelica was an effective remedy against the plague. Certainly, from early times it was used as such and was frequently grown in monastery gardens.

Chewing the stems is said to be a remedy for flatulence and a decoction of the root has been used to sooth hoarseness and sore throat and as a curative measure against typhus fever. An infusion of the leaves will ease smoker's cough and bronchitis. It also has a reputation for causing a distaste for alcohol.

Angelica, the happy
counter bane
Sent down from heaven
by some celestial scout
As well its name and
nature both avow't.

JOSHUA SYLVESTER

TO PRESERVE ANGELICA ROOTS

Wash them, slice them thin, put them to steep in fair Water, and shift the Water every day, for three Days. Then set them all night in a Pot over warm Embers, pour off the water in the Morning, and take two pounds of sugar and two Quarts of Water to a Pound of Roots, and boil them in it; when they are boil'd enough take them out and boil the Syrup gently.

The Receipt Book of John Nott, Cook to the Duke of Bolton, 1723

Angelica and Rhubarb Fool

1 lb (450g) rhubarb
4 tablespoons chopped angelica leaves
4 tablespoons red grape juice
4 tablespoons honey
3 egg yolks
7 fl oz (200ml) milk
vanilla pod
7 fl oz (200ml) thick cream
candied angelica for decoration

Chop the rhubarb. Put it into a saucepan with the angelica, grape juice and honey. Cover and set on a low heat for 15 minutes, or until the rhubarb is soft. Rub the contents of the pan through a sieve. Cool and chill.

Beat the egg yolks in a bowl. Put the milk into a saucepan with the vanilla pod and bring it slowly to the boil. Remove the vanilla pod. Quickly stir the milk into the egg yolks.

Put the custard mixture into a double saucepan or into a bowl standing in a pan of water. Stir over a low heat, without letting the water boil, until the mixture thickens. Cool and chill.

Lightly whip the thick cream. Fold it into the rhubarb purée. Fold in the custard. Put the fool either into one large dish or into individual bowls and chill for at least 15 minutes. Before serving, decorate with small pieces of candied angelica.

Serves 6

— SPECIAL USES —

Angelica was an ingredient in *Eau de Carmes*, or Carmelite Water, a famed toilet water and cordial invented by the Carmelite monks in Paris in 1611.

Formerly in household usage, the dried roots and seeds were burnt in pans to fumigate a musty room.

Laplanders have a custom of chewing angelica and smoking it like tobacco.

— LORE —

In Iceland and Scandinavia, angelica was believed to be of heavenly origin. The Letts believed it magical and chanted songs when it was carried to market as part of an ancient pagan festival. With Christianity, the festival became associated with the Annunciation. In many parts of northern Europe, angelica has been held to be effective against witchcraft and evil.

Basil

O C Y M U M B A S I L I U M

The sun-loving basil has been cultivated for at least four thousand years. It is a native of Asia and Africa which found its way through what is now Iran to ancient Greece and from thence to Italy and the rest of Europe, to Britain, North and South America and the Pacific Islands.

When sweet basil first reached England in the middle of the sixteenth century it was regarded mainly as a medicinal and a decorative plant. It soon found a place in Tudor and Stuart herb gardens, where it was grown mainly in containers: 'Basil is sowen in gardens in earthen pots' wrote Gervase Markham in 1613.

At this time, feelings were mixed towards the useful value of basil. Country housewives often made gifts of pots of basil as a compliment to visitors, but others associated it with evil. Later in the seventeenth century, the superstition was forgotten and records of 1726 show that up to fifty varieties were being cultivated in Britain.

Sweet or common basil has always been the main culinary variety, although lettuce-leaf basil, so-called because of its large leaves, comes a close second for flavour. The low-growing bush basil and attractive purple basil can also be used, although their flavours are slightly more resinous. There is a curled-leaved variety and one with narrow leaves and an aniseed scent. The smaller, sacred basil is sweet, pungent and spicy. Other species include lemon basil and camphor basil, and hedge or wild basil which grows wild in England and Scotland.

— CULTIVATION —

Culpeper instructed that basil 'must be sown late . . . it being a very tender plant', and this is still true. If basil is to be sown directly outside, wait until May when all the frosts are over. Better still, sow it in a large earthenware pot in early spring and keep it on a sunny windowsill or in a sun-filled conservatory. Keep it well watered, for it likes the damp as well as the heat.

Both the ancient Greeks and the Romans believed that the more basil was cursed and sworn at during the time of planting, the better it would grow. Despite this, germination is usually fairly quick. Thin out the plants in the pot by transferring about half to a sunny position in the herb garden. Keep the rest in the pot in a sunny spot near the house and make

sure both are well watered. Pinching out the flowers as soon as they appear encourages leafier plants.

Basil planted out of doors will die with the first frosts. Potted plants, however, can be taken inside into a warm kitchen and should provide you with fresh leaves all winter.

Basil will not seed itself in temperate climates and so must be resown each spring.

— CULINARY USES —

Basil appears in a late fourteenth-century French recipe for 'green pickle' and in a fifteenth-century English manuscript it is listed as one of the herbs 'for pottage'. In the seventeenth century it gave a characteristic flavour to a much-enjoyed type of sausage made in Fetter Lane, London. Mrs. Beeton used it to flavour Mock Turtle Shop and around the same time it was one of the principal herbs in an 'Aromatic Seasoning' devised by Francatelli, one-time cook to Queen Victoria.

Basil is a true herb of the sun, perfect accompaniment for tomatoes and other summer vegetables. A mere sprinkling over a tomato salad will work magic. Use it, too, in tomato soups and sauces, in ratatouille or a chilled gazpacho. The Italians add it to fish soups and pound it with pine nuts, garlic and Parmesan cheese to make pesto, a sauce for pasta. They add it to mayonnaise and preserve the leaves in oil for winter use. To preserve the flavour for winter salads, steep the leaves in a bottle of white wine vinegar.

'The smell of basil is good for the heart and for the head, that the seede cureth the infirmities of the heart, taketh away sorrowfulnesse which cometh of melancholy, and maketh a man merry and glad.'

JOHN GERARD, 1597

Tomato and Basil Sauce for Pasta

1 lb (450g) tomatoes
3 tablespoons olive oil
1 medium onion, finely chopped
1 garlic clove, finely chopped
3 tablespoons chopped basil
2 oz (50g) ground almonds
4 oz (125g) low-fat soft cheese

Scald, skin and chop the tomatoes. Heat the oil in a saucepan on a low heat. Put in the onion and garlic and cook them until they are soft and golden. Put in the tomatoes and basil. Cover and cook gently for 10 minutes, or until the tomatoes are very soft. Stir in the ground almonds and the cheese. Reheat gently but do not allow to boil.

Spoon the sauce over cooked spaghetti or tagliatelle, or any of the larger pasta shapes.

Serves 4

— MEDICINAL USES —

Old herbalists could never agree over basil. Some loved it but others were either frightened to use it, or regarded it as being of little medicinal use. In the seventeenth century, both Gerard and Parkinson recommended it 'to procure a cheerfull and merry hearte', but Culpeper mentions it merely as an antidote for the stings of 'venomous beasts'.

The dried leaves have been taken like snuff for migraines and nervous headaches. In South America, basil is used to purge intestinal parasites. The

infusion is a mild, non-toxic tranquillizer which has been recommended for nervousness, insomnia and stomach disorders of nervous origin.

The 'speakers' of the Fang tribes of Africa chew basil leaves to gain inspiration before their ritual ceremonies.

— LORE —

To the Hindus of India, sacred basil is the most sacred of all plants and it is planted on graves and around temples as well as in the home. It is thought to be a protection against evil and every Hindu is buried with a basil leaf on his breast.

In Greece there is a legend that basil was brought to Greece by the Empress Helena who found it on the site of the crucifixion; but another ancient Greek belief was that it represented hate, misfortune and poverty.

In Crete and in some parts of Italy it was a symbol of 'love washed with tears', as shown in the Boccaccio story of Isabella which was retold by Keats: Isabella planted basil in a pot containing the head of her dead lover, killed by her brothers, and wept over it. In other parts of Europe, basil was a love token, meant to secure the love of any person to whom it was given.

Some sixteenth and seventeenth century English herbalists were convinced that basil could breed scorpions and that even smelling the plant would cause venomous creatures to breed in one's brain.

Bay

L A U R U S   N O B I L I S

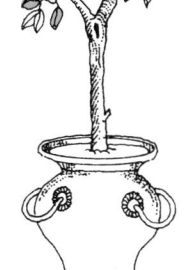

The evergreen bay tree grows wild in southern Spain, Morocco and around the eastern Mediterranean. It was well known to the ancient Greeks and Romans and the leaves were used to flavour savoury dishes and drinks in the kitchens of medieval Europe. It was not until Tudor times that the bay tree was cultivated in Britain, but by the early seventeenth century the bay was 'so well known, that it needs no description' (Culpeper).

— CULTIVATION —

The bay tree will grow in decorative tubs or in a sheltered spot in the garden, preferably where it is slightly shaded by other trees. Ideally, the soil should be well composted. Although it is an evergreen, bay is susceptible to hard frosts and to very cold winds, so it needs to be protected in the winter until it is well grown. Tubs can be taken indoors or sheltered under glass. Outdoor trees should be protected by being covered with clear plastic during the winter months. Should a young tree die in cold weather, new shoots will grow up within two months if the old wood is cut back.

The bay may be propagated by cuttings taken in midsummer. Each should have a 'heel' attached and

Custom has it that basil and rue should be kept apart in the herb garden, for each retards the other's growth.

Basil has a traditional use as a strewing herb to keep away flies, and was also an ingredient in sweet washing waters.

. . . neither witch nor devil, thunder nor lightning will hurt a man where a bay tree is.

NICHOLAS CULPEPER, 1652

should be dipped in rooting powder. Protection under glass encourages the cuttings to take quickly.

Bay trees in pots or tubs look most attractive if they are trained to grow on a single stem and the tops trimmed to spherical or pyramidal shapes.

Bay leaves can be gathered all year and used dry or fresh.

— CULINARY USES —

In medieval times bay leaves flavoured soups, meat jellies and wines. They were also used in sweet dishes and *The Goodman of Paris* (1393) gives a first course of 'cooked apples and large Provençal figs roasted, with bay leaves thereon'. Even today, dessert figs are still packaged together with a bay leaf to give a slight flavour and an attractive appearance.

A bay leaf is an essential part of a *bouquet garni*, and alone the leaves are indispensible for stocks, soups, sauces, marinades, casseroles and braised dishes, and boiled meats. New potatoes taste delicious when boiled with a bay leaf, as do carrots or artichokes.

Milk infused with bay makes superb white sauces and soufflés, as well as sweet rice puddings, blancmanges and custard tarts. Chilled, it provides a simple but refreshing drink.

Dried bay leaves are said to stimulate the appetite and so they are added to commercially produced pickles and sauces.

— MEDICINAL USES —

The leaves, berries and bark of bay have all been used medicinally since the time of Hippocrates. The whole tree was said to be effective against plague; during outbreaks of plague in Rome the people were advised to live in the vicinity of bay trees, in the place now known as San Lorenzo. In Tudor times in England, the leaves and berries were crushed and used in pomanders for the same reason.

An infusion of bay leaves or berries will restore lost appetite. A bath containing such an infusion has restorative powers and relieves aching limbs. It was also once thought to be a cure for colic. Oil of bay can be used as a rub for sprains and bruises. *Bankes' Herbal* of 1525 recommends a powder of the berries mixed with honey to take away red blemishes on the face.

Potatoes Baked with Bay

8 small potatoes
8 bay leaves
1½ oz (40g) butter

Heat the oven to 400°F/200°C/gas mark 6. With a sharp knife, make a deep slit in the long side of each potato, cutting about three-quarters of the way through. Insert a bay leaf as far as it will go into each slit.

Put the butter into an ovenproof dish. Melt it in the oven. Roll the potatoes in the butter, leaving them in the dish. Bake them for 1 hour 15 minutes.

A mild bay flavour will penetrate the potatoes.

Serves 4

It serveth to adorn the house of God, as well as of man; to procure warmth, comfort and strength to the limbs of men and women by bathings and annoyntings out and by drinks etc., inward; to season the vessels wherein are preserved our meates, as well as our drinkes; to crown or encircle as with a garland the heads of the living and to stick and decke forth the bodies of the dead; so that from the cradle to the grave we still have use of, we still have need of it.

JOHN PARKINSON, 1629

Bay was a strewing herb and its leaves were burned on an open fire to refresh and cleanse rooms. The oil from the berries is used in the manufacture of soap and perfume. The sweet-scented wood is used decoratively in marquetry and as fragrant fuel for the smoking of cheese and meat.

— LORE —

To the Greeks and Romans, bay was a sacred tree, dedicated to Apollo and to Aesculapius, the god of medicine. In Greece, the Delphic Oracle was decorated with the leaves. In Rome, the bay tree was an emblem of glory; victorious heroes, and winners of the games were crowned with wreaths of the leaves, as were young doctors. Branches were placed over the palace gates and letters announcing victory were wrapped in the leaves. Poets were also garlanded with laurel leaves and this is the origin of the title 'poet laureate'.

In England, from medieval to Stuart times, bay was thought to be a powerful antidote to witchcraft and branches were used to decorate houses and churches at Christmas.

Bergamot

M O N A R D A D I D Y M A

Bergamot flowers are particularly attractive to bees as they are rich in nectar.

The shaggy flowerheads of the refreshingly scented bergamot are a late summer delight in any herb garden. The most spectacular are the bright red varieties such as 'Cambridge Scarlet' or 'Prairie Fire'. The flowers of other types vary through creamy white and pink to purple and red. The scent is similar to that of the bergamot orange of Northern Italy, the oil of which is used for making eau de Cologne.

Bergamot is a native of the swampy areas of the United States and Canada, growing as far south as Georgia. It was first described in 1569 in a book on American flora by a Dr Nicholas Monardes of Seville, from whom the plant takes its botanical name. Accounts vary as to when bergamot was first taken to Europe, but it was probably cultivated in Britain from around the middle of the seventeenth century.

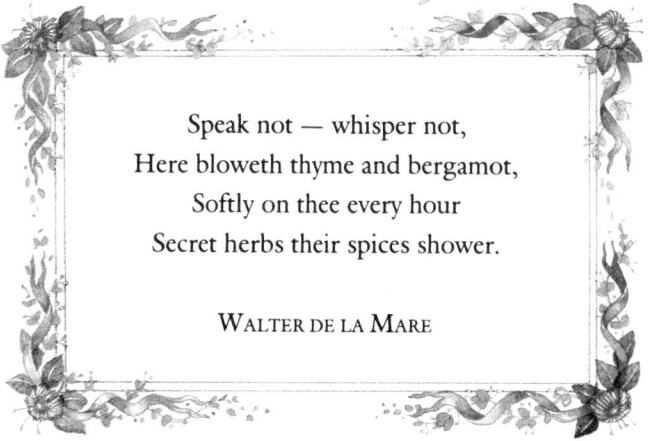

Speak not — whisper not,
Here bloweth thyme and bergamot,
Softly on thee every hour
Secret herbs their spices shower.

WALTER DE LA MARE

— CULTIVATION —

Bergamot will grow up to 3 feet (1 metre) high, so place it near the back of the herb garden. It flourishes whether it is in full sun or partial shade, but the soil must be kept moist and well composted. A planting area beside a stream or a water garden would be an ideal spot.

Bergamot is best propagated by root division either in spring or in early autumn. Every three years, dig up the plants, discard the old centre parts and replant the younger sections in fresh soil, about 2 feet (60cm) apart.

Trim established plants back every autumn to a height of about 3 inches (7.5cm) to encourage thick new growth in the spring.

— CULINARY USES —

The American Indians gathered wild bergamot, which they called Oswego, to make a refreshing tea and that has been its chief use ever since. Bergamot was cultivated in most early American gardens and the tea was drunk by the colonists in great quantities around the time of the Boston Tea Party.

In eighteenth and nineteenth century England, bergamot was grown for the same purpose, many people preferring its flavour to that of China or Indian tea. The famous Earl Grey tea is now made by adding oil of bergamot, made from the bergamot orange, to Indian tea, but you can obtain a similarly refreshing taste by adding some chopped bergamot leaves to your favourite blend of Indian or China tea.

Try also infusing the leaves in light white wines or mixtures of fruit juices and in summer fruit cups.

The refreshing, orange-like flavour of bergamot leaves makes them a good addition to salads and stuffings. Add them to mixtures of herbs and garlic for cream or curd cheeses and to *bouquets garnis* for meat dishes, particularly pork, veal, beef and lamb.

— MEDICINAL USES —

Bergamot tea is soothing and relaxing and so makes a good night-time drink. Add a handful of fresh leaves to your bath to sooth tired and aching limbs.

— SPECIAL USES —

The dried leaves, stems and roots of bergamot give a sharp, refreshing scent to a dry pot-pourri and the crushed leaves can be added with rose petals to a pot-pourri made by the moist method.

Bergamot and Orange Warmer

4 tablespoons chopped bergamot leaves
grated rind and juice of 2 medium-sized oranges
20 floz (575ml) boiling water
honey

Put the bergamot leaves and orange rind and juice into a teapot. Pour on the boiling water. Cover and keep warm and leave to brew for 10 minutes. Strain into cups. Sweeten with honey to taste, if required.

Borage

BORAGO OFFICINALIS

The rough, hairy-leaved borage with its weird black-centred, deep blue flowers has been known since ancient times. It is a native of the Mediterranean area and was taken by the Romans to many parts of Europe and Britain where it quickly became naturalized. Early settlers took borage to North America, where also it can now be found growing wild.

It has a very old reputation as a bringer of courage. Some say its name comes from the old Celtic name *borrach* which means courage, or from the Latin *cor ago*, meaning 'I stimulate the heart'. The Arabs called it *abourach* for quite different reasons. In their language it meant 'father of sweat', a reference to its medicinal properties.

— CULTIVATION —

Borage will grow anywhere and everywhere, although it does prefer a sunny position in a light, well-drained soil. The seed can be sown in early to mid spring or midsummer. Sow thinly and thin out the plants to about 18 inches (45cm) apart. The plants are rather top-heavy with small roots and so cannot be transplanted, but once you have sown borage in the herb garden you will never be without it, for it readily seeds itself and comes up in the most unexpected of places. It can grow up to 3 feet (1 metre) in height, so remove any plants that will mask others from the light.

Cut the plants back after flowering and remove any dead leaves. Pull up all old plants after the first late autumn frosts.

— CULINARY USES —

The ancient Greeks and Romans put borage leaves into wine cups to give a refreshing, cucumber-like fragrance. In eighteenth-century England one of the plant's common names was Cool Tankard, referring to the same use, and today certain cocktails are not complete without a borage leaf. Fruit juices and iced lemon tea benefit equally.

The other uses of borage, however, seem to have been forgotten. It was originally a valued pot-herb and the

Here is sweet water and borage for blending, Comfort and courage to drink at your will.

N. HOPPER

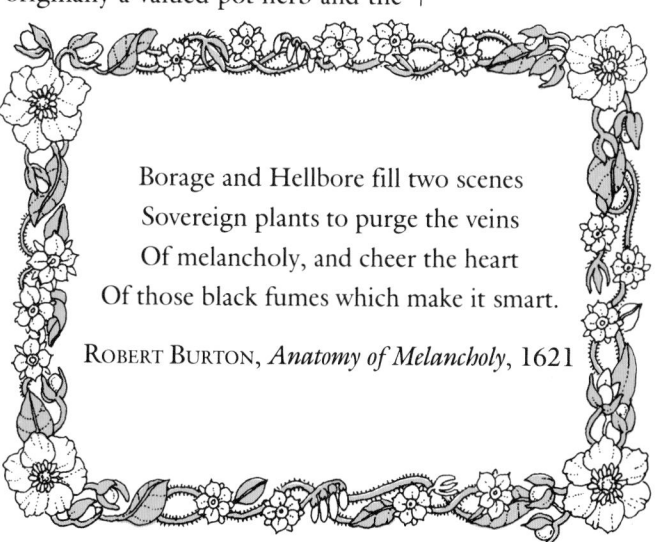

Borage and Hellbore fill two scenes
Sovereign plants to purge the veins
Of melancholy, and cheer the heart
Of those black fumes which make it smart.

ROBERT BURTON, *Anatomy of Melancholy*, 1621

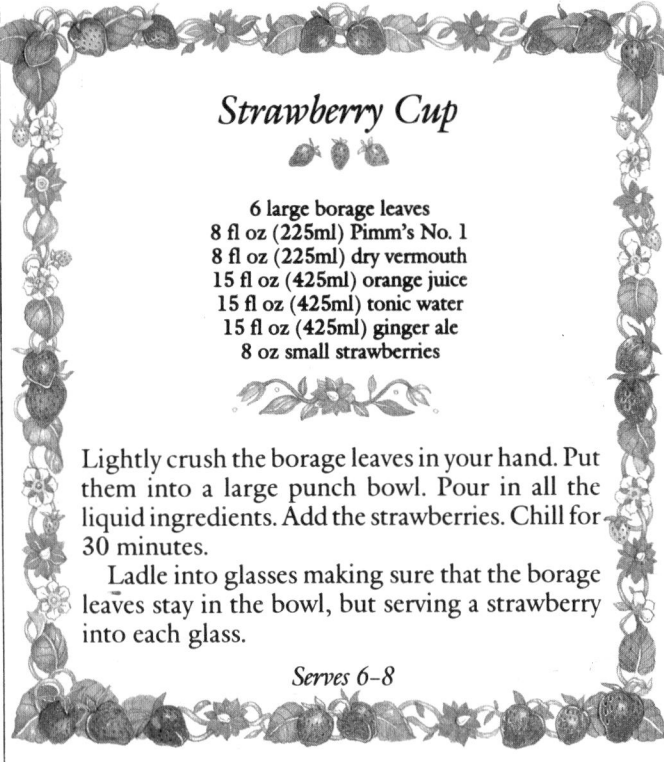

Strawberry Cup

6 large borage leaves
8 fl oz (225ml) Pimm's No. 1
8 fl oz (225ml) dry vermouth
15 fl oz (425ml) orange juice
15 fl oz (425ml) tonic water
15 fl oz (425ml) ginger ale
8 oz small strawberries

Lightly crush the borage leaves in your hand. Put them into a large punch bowl. Pour in all the liquid ingredients. Add the strawberries. Chill for 30 minutes.

Ladle into glasses making sure that the borage leaves stay in the bowl, but serving a strawberry into each glass.

Serves 6–8

Its flowers putt into broth give a special taste, and taken in wine they cause great joy and fearlessness.

The Herbal of Renodaeus

young tops were often used to flavour soup. The flowers were candied and made into syrups and cordials and the young leaves were chopped into salads. In parts of southern England in the eighteenth and nineteenth centuries, a few borage leaves were eaten with the ploughman's lunch of bread and cheese and cider.

Borage flowers make a superb garnish for salads and cold dishes. You can make fritters with the whole leaves, or chop and mix them into stuffings or cream cheese.

— MEDICINAL USES —

Borage has always been known as a herb to bring courage, one which can 'exhilarate and make the minde glad', and it was mainly for this reason that it was first used in drinks and salads. With rose, violet and anchusa, it was considered by the ancients to be one of the most important cordial herbs which would cheer the heart. John Pechey in his *Herbal* of 1695 said it would 'comfort the heart, relieve the faint, cheer the melancholy, and purify the blood'. John Evelyn in *Acetaria*, 1699 recommended it to 'revive the hypochondriac and cheer the hard student'.

A decoction or infusion of borage has long been recommended to bring on sweating and so it has been given for fevers, chills, measles, and influenza and feverish colds. The crushed dried leaves, together with those of dandelion and watercress, were once sold by apothecaries in springtime as a blood cleansing tonic.

— SPECIAL USES —

Borage flowers are loved by bees and pollen from them produces excellent honey. In Tudor and Stuart times, the strange but attractive flowers were a very popular motif in women's needlework designs.

— LORE —

The courage-giving properties of borage were very much magnified in early times. In medieval England, infusions of the flowers and leaves were drunk before jousting tournaments.

The leaves and flowers of Borage comforteth the heart, purgeth melancholy, and quieteth the phrenticke or lunaticke person.

JOHN GERARD, 1597

Chamomile

C H A M A E M E L U M   N O B I L E

In Tudor England, chamomile was a symbol of humility and patience.

You will always know that you have walked over chamomile because its daisy-like flowers and bright green leaves will immediately give off their rich, fruity aroma. Its name comes from Greek words meaning 'earth apple' and the Spanish still call it Manzanilla, meaning 'little apple'.

In Anglo-Saxon Europe, chamomile was known as maythen and was one of the nine sacred herbs. Long before this, the Egyptians had dedicated the plant to their gods. It is indigenous to Britain and Europe and since early Norman times has always been grown in herb gardens. Chamomile lawns were popular in Tudor and Stuart England and it was on one of these that Sir Francis Drake was said to have played his famous game of bowls before fighting the Spanish Armada.

Chamomile for medicinal purposes was cultivated on a large scale at the beginning of this century in Belgium and France and also in the south of England and on the outskirts of London.

There are two types of chamomile, the perennial, common or Roman, *Chamaemelum nobile* and the German chamomile, *Matricaria chamomilla*. They have similar properties, although some herbalists maintain that the common chamomile is the most effective medicinally.

— CULTIVATION —

The German chamomile is an annual that can be grown from seed in spring or autumn. Prepare a firm, moist seed bed and sow in drills. When the plants are about 2 inches (5cm) high, thin

A rinse of chamomile flowers gives highlights to blonde hair.

It delights the mind and brings health to the body.

WILLIAM LAWSON,
1617

All parts of this excellent plant are of virtue.

SIR JOHN HILL, 1772

them out to about 6 inches (15cm) apart in a sunny part of the herb garden. German chamomile is not suitable for lawns.

The common or perennial chamomile can be grown either from seed or by dividing the plants in late spring or early autumn. It can be cultivated as a low edging for a herb garden, in the cracks between paving stones, or as a lawn. The saying is that 'the more it is trodden, the faster it grows' and so chamomile can even flourish when grown as a path. In old herb gardens, banks and raised seats were covered with chamomile to make a fragrant resting place.

A chamomile lawn or other patch of perennial chamomile should be regularly weeded until it is well established. To ensure that it grows thick and green, cut it back to prevent it from flowering and roll it at regular intervals.

— CULINARY USES —

Chamomile is mostly used to make a soothing tea. Manzanilla sherry is flavoured with chamomile and this can be served at the beginning of a meal accompanied by a bowl of olives. Chamomile is also an ingredient of herb beer.

— MEDICINAL USES —

Chamomile tea has long been known as a mild sedative. It has been administered to help sleep, to calm nervousness and hysteria, to relieve nervous indigestion, to prevent nightmares and to cut short *delirium tremens*. A very mild tea can soothe fractious babies.

A warmed bag of dried chamomile soothes earache and eases neuralgia. Steeped in boiling water, it is soothing to facial swellings caused by abcesses.

Culpeper recommended chamomile for jaundice and dropsy, and when first introduced into the United States it was used as a poultice to prevent gangrene.

— SPECIAL USES —

Chamomile was a strewing herb, used particularly at weddings, and it was boiled with orange peel to make washing waters for the table. The dried leaves were either smoked or taken as snuff as a cure for sleeplessness.

Sherry Cooler

10 fl oz (275ml) medium sherry
4 chamomile sprigs
10 fl oz (275ml) orange juice
4 orange slices
8 ice cubes

Infuse the sherry with the chamomile in a covered jug in a warm place for 2 hours. Remove the chamomile. Pour in the chilled orange juice.

Cut each orange slice in half. Put two halves into each of four tall glasses and add two ice cubes to each glass. Pour in the sherry and orange juice.

Chervil

CHOEROPHYLLUM SATIVUM

Chervil is a delicate plant with finely cut, lacy green leaves which fade to a pinky colour after the small clusters of tiny white flowers have dropped, leaving their long seeds. Its flavour and scent are mildly aniseed with a hint of parsley. There are two types of chervil, *Choerophyllum sativum* and *Anthriscus cerefolium*, but they are so very similar that they are always thought of as one plant.

Chervil is a native of south-eastern Europe and western Asia, but it is now naturalized in every continent. It has been used and loved since ancient times and is thought to be one of the warming spices that was used to make the oil with which Moses blessed the vessels of the Tabernacle. The Romans took chervil to Britain and ever since it has grown there by hedges and waysides as well as in herb gardens. Early settlers took it to America.

The botanical name, *Choerophyllum*, comes from Greek words meaning 'that which warms the heart'.

— CULTIVATION —

Chervil is an annual that can be sown in early spring, or in late summer for a longer season the following year. It readily seeds itself so, once grown, there should be no need to replant. In fact, it can spread its seeds over a wide area and may have to be checked if it spreads too far. It quickly runs to seed if transplanted, so sow the seed thinly in drills 12 inches (30cm) apart and thin the plants within the rows if necessary. You can also sow it as a pretty edging to a herb garden or flower border.

Where the climate is cool, chervil is at its best in the summer. In hotter climates, the best foliage grows from autumn to spring. You may well find that after producing lush growth in the spring, it will die back during the hotter months only to flourish again in the autumn.

As the plants are so delicate, it is best to snip off leaves with scissors rather than attempting to break off sprigs.

— CULINARY USES —

Chervil has always been used far more in Europe than in Britain or the United States. The French have enjoyed it since early times and it has also been a favourite seasoning plant in Holland. Both Gerard in 1597 and Parkinson in 1629 describe a type of stew known as a Loblolly, made in Holland, in which chervil was used as a seasoning. The French have also frequently used its distinctive flavour

in soups and casseroles.

In medieval times, chervil was used as a salad herb and pottage herb and it frequently featured in the sauces that were used to make Lenten food more interesting. In Tudor and Stuart times in England, its long tap roots were boiled and candied.

Today, with tarragon, chives and parsley, chervil is one of the *fines herbes* that marry so beautifully with omelettes. Even by itself, chervil is a superb 'egg herb'. It also goes well with fish and in stuffings for chicken or veal and enhances many vegetables, particularly carrots, when sprinkled over them before serving. A sprig can be used to flavour milk for sweet puddings and custards. It is used commercially for flavouring liqueurs.

— MEDICINAL USES —

It is said that chervil will improve both the digestion and the appetite. It helps to cleanse the blood and is a mild diuretic. An infusion or decoction washed over the face will help to remove blemishes.

Culpeper, in 1649, recommended a fomentation of chervil for bruises and swellings. Parkinson recommended the candied roots to 'warme and comfort a phlegmaticke stomack' and also as a protection against plague.

Mackerel with Chervil

4 medium-sized mackerel
4 tablespoons chopped chervil
4 tablespoons olive oil
juice of half a lemon
1 teaspoon mustard powder
lemon wedges
sprigs of chervil

Clean the mackerel. Cut the tails into neat V-shapes. The heads can be left on or cut off, whichever is preferred. Cut three diagonal slits on each side of the mackerel, running downwards from head to tail. Lay the mackerel on a large, flat dish.

Mix together the chervil, oil, lemon juice and mustard powder. Rub the mixture over the mackerel, making sure some gets into the slits and the body cavity. Cover and leave for 4 hours at room temperature.

When you are ready to cook, heat the grill to high and if you have an open wire rack, cover it with foil. Lay the mackerel on the hot rack and grill them until golden brown on each side, about 10 minutes altogether.

Serve garnished with lemon wedges and sprigs of chervil.

Serves 4

Chives

A L L I U M   S C H O E N O P R A S U M

Chive flowers, fresh or dried, make an attractive addition to a flower arrangement.

Chives have been called 'The Little Brothers of the Onion' and that, in effect, is what they are. They have small, spiky, onion-like leaves, a delicate onion scent and flavour, and similar flowers that burst out of their buds to become a riot of pink-purple pompoms. In country areas, they have been called chibboles or chibbals, and in Tudor times, seithes, sieves, sweth, civet and rush-leek, a rough translation of their Latin name.

Chives are known to have been grown and used by the ancient Chinese three thousand years before Christ, and for many years they have grown wild over most of the northern hemisphere, including Siberia, North America, southern Sweden, Greece and Corsica. The Romans took them to Britain where they can now be found wild in the northern and western countries, and since that time they have been grown almost unceasingly in cottage gardens.

— CULTIVATION —

Chives enjoy a good, rich soil in full sun, but they will really grow well under almost any conditions. They look pretty in large pots, tubs and barrels and make an ideal edging for a herb garden. Wherever you decide to place them, keep them well weeded, taking particular care to remove any couch grass that springs up in the middle; enrich their soil with a good compost and keep them watered.

Chives can be grown from seed or propagated by dividing the roots of established plants either in midsummer after they have flowered, or in the autumn. They are perennial plants which die back completely in the winter but are among the first to send out new growth in early spring. The leaves grow best if plants are not allowed to flower, but it is not worth missing their bright show of colour in late spring. Trim away the flower stalks after flowering and water well during the summer to encourage new growth. If you do so the plants may well flower again in early autumn.

— CULINARY USES —

Wherever you need just a hint of onion flavour instead of the strength of large onions, use chives. Sprinkle them into salads or over soups, add them to savoury butters, to cream or cottage cheese or to soured cream or

Chive Pancakes

For the batter:
4 oz (125g) wholewheat flour
4 tablespoons chopped chives
4 tablespoons chopped parsley
pinch salt
1 egg
1 egg yolk
1 tablespoon sunflower oil
5 fl oz (150ml) milk
5 fl oz (150ml) water
oil for shallow frying

For the filling:
8 oz (225g) cottage cheese
3 oz (75g) Double Gloucester or mild Cheddar cheese, grated
4 tablespoons chopped chives
1 egg, beaten

For the topping:
2 oz (50g) Double Gloucester or mild Cheddar cheese
2 tablespoons chopped chives

Put the flour in a bowl with the chives, parsley and salt. Make a well in the centre. Put in the egg and egg yolk and gradually beat in flour from the sides of the well. Add the oil and beat in the milk and water. Beat to make a smooth batter. Leave it in a cool place for 30 minutes. Use it to make 8 pancakes.

Heat the oven to 400°F/200°C/gas mark 6. Mix together the ingredients for the filling. Put a portion into each pancake and roll it up. Lay the pancakes in an oven-proof dish. Mix together the ingredients for the topping. Scatter them over the pancakes. Put the pancakes into the oven for 20 minutes.

yoghurt for a popular topping for baked potatoes.

Chives go well in egg dishes and with chervil, tarragon and parsley, make up *fines herbes*.

Add them to beefburgers for extra flavour or sprinkle them over steak after grilling. They are said to make fatty meats more digestible.

If you find that your chives are spreading too far over your herb garden, dig up some of the plants and pickle the small bulbs like onions. The flowers are also edible and taste slightly stronger than the leaves. They make a pretty garnish for starters, salads and other cold dishes.

— MEDICINAL USES —

Chives are thought to stimulate the appetite so they have been mixed into egg dishes for invalids. They are mildly antibiotic and have a reputation for strengthening the stomach.

With their iron and sulphur content, chives make an excellent general tonic and blood cleanser. They are thought to help reduce blood pressure and to be beneficial to the kidneys.

In ancient China, chives were used as an antidote to poisons and to staunch bleeding.

Culpeper did not care for chives and nearly omitted them from his Herbal of 1649, saying: 'I confess I had not added these had it not been for a country gentleman, who by a letter certified to me that amongst other herbs I had left these out'. He thought that 'they send up very hurtful vapours to the brain, causing troublesome sleep and spoiling the eyesight.'

Comfrey

SYMPHITUM OFFICINALE

The tall comfrey plant, with its large, thick, hairy leaves and hanging, bell-like flowers in various shades of pink and purple, flourishes by water. It is said that it grows on the sites of ancient fords and ferries where it was often employed in treating wounded travellers. There is a story of a locks-man at Teddington, on the Thames near London, who crushed his little finger. A doctor instructed him to chew comfrey root and also to bind it on his finger and he was completely cured in four days.

These healing powers of comfrey have been known since ancient times and it is said to have been named by the Greek physician Dioscorides nearly two thousand years ago. *Symphitum* comes from the Greek *sympho*, meaning 'to unite.' Comfrey is a corruption of the Latin *confervere*, meaning 'to grow together'. Its country names include Knit-Bone, Bruise-Wort, Church Bells and Ass-Ear, referring to the shape of its leaves.

Comfrey grows wild all through Europe, as far east as Siberia, and also in the mid-western and eastern States of America.

— CULTIVATION —

Comfrey prefers a damp, rich soil in partial shade. It can be grown from seed but is best propagated by root division in the autumn. Take pieces about 4 inches (10cm) long and set them about 18 inches (45cm) apart under about 1 inch (2.5cm) of soil: they will sprout readily. Comfrey roots are very brittle, so take care not to break them while digging near the plants if you do not want your comfrey patch to spread rapidly. The plants will benefit from a dressing of compost or well-rotted manure in the spring.

— CULINARY USES —

The large, hairy leaves of comfrey do not look very appetizing, but when they are cooked they become soft and tender and have a delicate flavour. They can be boiled for 12 minutes and served with melted butter, or stir-braised, by turning them in melted butter, adding 5 fl oz (150ml) water per 1 lb (450g) and simmering for 15 minutes. Once cooked, comfrey can be chopped and added to white sauce or a souffle.

The larger leaves makes superb fritters and the young shoots can be blanched and braised like celery. Chopped raw leaves can be added to soups or made into tea. Even the roots can be boiled as a vegetable, or alternatively dried and ground and used like coffee.

— MEDICINAL USES —

The chief use of comfrey since ancient times has been its medicinal one. Its powers of healing wounds, stopping

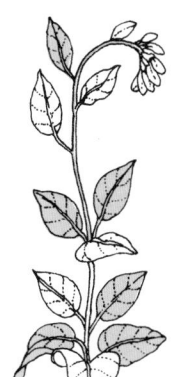

Lay comfrey leaves in your potato trenches for a bumper, superbly flavoured crop.

This is the Consound, Whereby the lungs are eased of their grief.

TENNYSON

... yea, it is said to be so powerful to consolidate and knit together, that if they be boiled with dissevered pieces of flesh in a pot, it will join them together again.

NICHOLAS CULPEPER, 1649

bleeding, easing sprains and mending bones are famous. Decoctions and infusions are effective in curing stomach ulcers and in the treatment of lung disorders and whooping cough. A decoction in the bath water will soothe a tender skin and ease eczema.

— LORE —

There is an old belief that when using comfrey medicinally, plants with cream-coloured flowers should be used for a woman and those with purple flowers for a man.

In the Middle Ages it was thought that a strong decoction of comfrey in the bath would restore lost virginity. This was tried to good effect by a servant girl. Her mistress, not wanting to waste the hot water, unknowingly climbed in after her, much to the surprise of her husband.

Chopped comfrey added to the feed is said to increase the laying of hens.

Deep Fried Comfrey Leaves with Parsley Mayonnaise

8 large, thick comfrey leaves

For the batter:
4 oz (125g) wholewheat flour
pinch salt
1 egg, separated
1 tablespoon sunflower oil
8 fl oz (225ml) bitter beer
oil for deep frying

For the mayonnaise:
1 egg yolk
½ teaspoon mustard powder
4 fl oz (125ml) sunflower oil
juice of half a lemon
6 tablespoons chopped parsley

Leave 1 inch (2.5cm) of stalk on the leaves.

To make the mayonnaise, put the egg yolk into a bowl. Add the mustard powder and beat them together. Add 2 tablespoons of oil, drop by drop. Beat in 2 teaspoons of lemon juice and finally the rest of the oil, a little at a time. Add extra lemon juice to taste. Put the mayonnaise into a liquidizer with the parsley. Work to a smooth, green sauce.

To make the batter, put the flour and salt into a bowl and make a well in the centre. Put in the egg yolk and oil and gradually bring in flour from the sides of the well. Beat in the beer, a little at a time. Leave the batter in a cool place for 30 minutes. Just before cooking, stiffly whip the egg white and fold it into the batter.

Heat a pan of deep oil to 350°F/180°C. Coat the comfrey leaves in the batter. Hold the stalk in one hand and the tip in the other. Lay the leaves in the hot batter, one at a time, and cook for 2 minutes on each side. Drain on kitchen paper.

Serves 4 as a first course

 # Coriander

C O R I A N D R U M   S A T I V U M

Grow coriander and there will always be a corner of your herb garden that is highly aromatic, especially in the hot sun, whether you are harvesting the deeply cut, shiny green leaves or the small, round green seeds.

Coriander is a native of southern Europe, North Africa and the Middle East. It was grown and used by the ancient Greeks and by the Egyptians, who passed on their knowledge of it to the Hebrews, for whom it was one of the bitter herbs of the Passover. The Talmud has many references to coriander, both as medicine and as food and it is one of the few medicinal plants that has been identified listed on eighth-century Babylonian clay tablets.

Coriander was taken to Britain by the Romans and was grown and used there in the Middle Ages. It was once grown commercially in Essex and Kent and may now be occasionally found there in the wild. Early settlers took coriander to America. It is also cultivated in India, but the best seed has always come from Egypt and North Africa.

Some people love the scent of fresh coriander and others dislike it. It is certainly very strong and pungent, yet it has a hint of pleasant freshness. The dried seeds are sweeter and more mellow.

— CULTIVATION —

Coriander is an annual that should be grown from seed in spring in an open, sunny situation. It prefers a warm, light, dry soil and flourishes beside chervil and dill. Either broadcast the seeds or sow them thinly in drills 8 inches (20cm) apart and thin to 4 inches (10cm). Its long roots make it difficult to transplant. Coriander germinates quickly and you should be able to use the leaves within five weeks. Harvest the seeds in late summer and lay them to dry in a warm place for a few days before storing in air-tight jars. As you harvest, scatter some seeds on the ground to save you the job of resowing in spring.

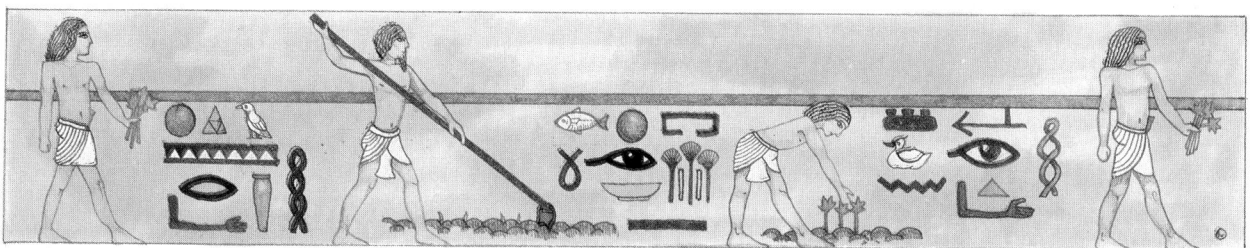

Lamb with Coriander

1½ lb (675g) lean, boneless lamb
1 large onion
4 tablespoons olive oil
1 garlic clove, chopped
1 teaspoon ground cumin
1 teaspoon ground coriander
2 teaspoons paprika
½ teaspoon cayenne pepper
7 fl oz (200ml) stock
2 tablespoons tomato puree
juice of half a lemon
4 tablespoons chopped fresh coriander

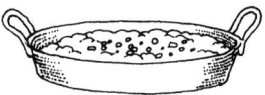

Cut the lamb into ¾ inch (2cm) cubes. Thinly slice the onion. Heat the oil in a large frying pan on a high heat. Put in the lamb, brown it and remove it. Lower the heat. Add the onion and garlic and soften them. Sprinkle in the cumin, coriander, paprika and cayenne pepper. Pour in the stock and bring it to the boil. Stir in the tomato puree. Replace the lamb. Cover and cook on a low heat for 30 minutes or until the lamb is tender and most of the stock has evaporated.

Mix in the lemon juice and half the chopped coriander. Serve with the remaining coriander sprinkled over the top.

Serves 4

— CULINARY USES —

Fresh coriander leaves can be used as a garnish in similar ways to parsley, but if you are using them chopped to scatter over cooked dishes be much more sparing. They are delicious with the spicy dishes of the Middle East and the curries and chutneys of India, and in China they are scattered over meat dishes just before serving. Fresh coriander is used extensively in Latin-American cooking added to meat dishes and chutneys and as garnish.

It is, however, the dried seeds that are used most frequently. They are an essential ingredient in most Indian curry dishes and in the spice mixture known as garam masala. In northern Europe and also in Egypt, ground or whole coriander seeds are added to certain breads. Ground coriander is a valuable ingredient for cakes, spiced biscuits and fruit pies.

Use the whole seeds as a pickling spice either for vinegar pickles or when preserving olives or salty cheese in oil. Use them to flavour ratatouille, beef casseroles or orange marmalade, or infuse them in milk before making junket or rice pudding.

Commercially, coriander seeds are combined with juniper to give flavour to gin and are used to improve the flavour of cocoa. At one time they were coated with sugar as sweetmeats for children.

— MEDICINAL USES —

An infusion of coriander seeds has been used for many years for indigestion and flatulence and at one time,

CORIANDER WATER

Take a handful of coriander seeds, break them and put them into about a quart of water, and so let it stand, put in a quarter of a pound of sugar, and when your sugar is melted and the water well taken the taste of the seeds, then strain it out through a cloath and drink it at your pleasure.

A Perfect School of Instruction for the Offices of the Month by Giles Rose, one of the Master Cooks to Charles II of England, 1682

sweetened with honey, it was thought to be a cure for worms.

The seeds have been an essential ingredient in many toilet waters, including the famous Carmelite water, invented by Carmelite monks in Paris in 1611. These toilet waters have had a variety of uses including cleansing and beautifying the skin. In many Eastern countries, preparations made from coriander seeds have been used for lightening the complexion.

William Turner, in 1551, advised: 'Coriandre layd to wyth breade or barly mele is good for Saynt Antonyes fyre' (erysipelas, a skin disease).

Coriander is now mainly used to mask the unpleasant taste of some medicines.

— LORE —

In ancient China, it was thought that anyone who ate coriander would enjoy immortality.

In the Middle East and in Europe, coriander has been valued as a love potion and aphrodisiac. It was one of the ingredients in the love potion prepared by the hashish seller in the story of Ala-al-Din Abu-al in the Arabian Nights, and an old European herbal says that it will have the power to induce love if it is gathered in the last quarter of the moon.

Another belief is that if coriander is burnt with black poppy, fennel, sandalwood and henbane, it will produce a whole army of demons.

Dill

A N E T H U M   G R A V E O L E N S

A pleasant and fragrant plant.

VIRGIL

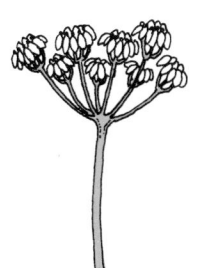

Dill is grown for its delicate, feathery leaves and also for its flat brown seeds, both of which have a pungent, savoury scent. It has long had a reputation for being a soothing, sedative herb and its name comes from the Saxon *dillan* and the Norse *dilla*, both of which mean 'to lull'.

Dill is native to the Mediterranean regions and to southern Russia. It grows wild in Spanish and Portuguese cornfields and along the coast of Italy and is widely cultivated throughout the world.

The first known mention of dill is in a five thousand year old Egyptian list of herbs. It was used medicinally by the Egyptians and was valued in Palestine at the time of Christ. The Romans took dill to Britain. It was used in Saxon times and by the fifteenth century was a common herb in kitchen gardens, grown for culinary

Therewith her Vervain and her Dill,
That hindereth Witches of their will.

DRAYTON, *Nymphidia*, seventeenth century

and medicinal use and as a powerful charm against witchcraft and evil.

Early settlers took dill to America where the seeds became known as 'meeting-house seeds', as people often chewed them to keep away hunger pangs and rumbling stomachs during the long sermons at Sunday services.

— CULTIVATION —

Dill is an annual. Sow the seeds in spring in a slightly moist but well-drained soil, either broadcast thinly or in drills 9 inches (22cm) apart. Dill grows well near to chervil and coriander, but do not sow it close to fennel as they may cross-pollinate to produce hybrid plants with little flavour. Water well in dry weather.

Some people prefer to sow the seeds in succession until midsummer to ensure a good supply of fresh leaves but, provided the soil is kept moist, one sowing should be enough. Harvest the seeds as soon as they ripen in late summer or early autumn.

— CULINARY USES —

Since the sixteenth century, and perhaps even earlier, dill leaves and seeds have been the chief flavouring ingredient for pickled cucumbers and gherkins, in Britain and Europe. It has also been favoured for making herb vinegars.

Dill is a popular herb in Scandinavia, where the fresh sprigs flavour the raw salmon dish knows as gravadlax. It is also good with conventionally cooked fish. Add chopped dill to soups and sauces and put a sprig in the saucepan with new potatoes.

The chopped leaves make an excellent addition to cool summer salads, to mayonnaise, yoghurt dressings and to cream or cottage cheese.

Dill seeds have a slightly stronger flavour. In France they are added to bread, cakes, apple pies and sauces, and small biscuits made for babies to chew on. They make an excellent flavouring for cabbage and for some stew-type dishes and strongly flavoured soups.

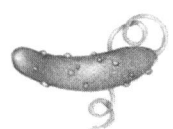

Salmon Salad with Dill

1½ lb (675g) fresh salmon fillets
freshly ground black pepper
4 dill sprigs
4 fl oz (125ml) dry white wine
1 oz (25g) butter

For the garnish:
4 dill sprigs
1 cucumber

For the mayonnaise:
make as for parsley mayonnaise (page 34), adding
2 tablespoons chopped dill with the parsley

Heat the oven to 400°F/200°C/gas mark 6. Skin the salmon fillets and cut them into four pieces. Lay them in an ovenproof dish. Season them with pepper and put a dill sprig on each piece. Pour in the wine and dot the fillets with butter. Cover with foil and bake for 20 minutes. Cool the salmon, still covered, in the dish.

Remove the dill sprigs. Lay the salmon fillets on a serving plate. Garnish them with fresh dill sprigs. Thinly slice the cucumber and arrange the slices round the salmon. Serve with mayonnaise.

— MEDICINAL USES —

A mild infusion of dill seeds is a tried and tested remedy for calming babies and getting rid of wind. In Saxon times it was rubbed on the breast after feeding the baby to lull it to sleep. The leaves and seeds are said to increase milk flow if taken daily by nursing mothers.

Dill water has also been used to sweeten bad breath and a few chopped leaves added to a daily salad will strengthen the hair and nails. The ground roasted seeds were once used as a cure for wounds and ulcers.

— SPECIAL USES —

The Greeks burnt dill seeds as a form of incense. Oil of dill is now used for perfuming soaps.

— LORE —

Dill has long had a reputation for protecting against witchcraft and evil. It was also, however, used by witches in spells and charms.

It is a plant of good omen and in some European countries the bride once put a sprig of dill and some salt in her shoes, as well as wearing a sprig on her dress.

Fennel

F O E N I C U L U M   V U L G A R E

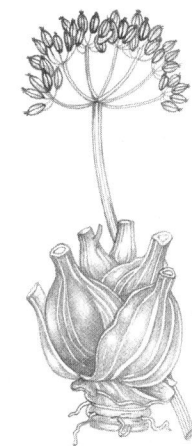

Fennel is a tall, stately plant with large, excessively finely cut, feathery leaves, which gradually droop backwards as they grow. Both the leaves and the small brown seeds have an aniseed-like taste, but somehow fresher. The Romans thought fennel smelt like fresh-cut hay and so came the Latin name of *Foeniculum, foenum* meaning hay. In the Middle Ages this became fanculum, then fenkel and later fennel.

Fennel is a native of the Mediterranean shores but it quickly became naturalized wherever it was taken, both eastwards to India, west all over Europe and Britain and eventually to America. It grows best near the sea and on chalky soil inland.

Fennel is mentioned in the writings on papyrus of ancient Egypt and was one of the herbs used medicinally by Hippocrates. Greek athletes training for their Olympic Games ate fennel to give them strength and to keep down weight. It was taken to Northern Europe and to Britain by the Romans and later was one of the nine sacred herbs of the Anglo-Saxons, who used it in cooking and as medicine.

In medieval Europe and Britain, fennel was valued by the poor who chewed it on fast days to allay hunger pangs. It was equally valued in the richest homes. The Emperor Charlemagne ordered its cultivation in all the imperial herb gardens of Europe. In 1281 the household of Edward I of England used 8½ lb (4kg) of fennel seed in one month.

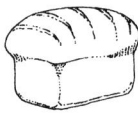

Fennel was introduced to America in the eighteenth century by Spanish priests and it can still be found growing wild on the sites of old missions. It was later grown commercially by the Shakers.

There are two types of fennel, common fennel which has bright green leaves, and bronze fennel, often grown as a decorative plant. Both have the same scent, flavour and properties.

— CULTIVATION —

Fennel is one of the easiest of herbs to grow. It will thrive in almost any soil and one plant will last for years, providing all the leaves and seeds that you will ever need.

It can be grown from seed in spring and then transplanted in midsummer. Put plants at the back of the herb garden, for fennel grows very tall and bushy, and give them plenty of space. If possible plant them in full sun.

Fennel leaves can be picked from an established plant from spring until late autumn. Harvest the seeds in early autumn. Cut the plant right back in the autumn to encourage new growth in the following spring.

— CULINARY USES —

Fennel has a centuries-old reputation of being an excellent herb with fish, partly because of the flavour and partly because it is supposed to counteract the richness of oily fish.

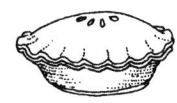

Whiting with Lemon and Fennel

4 medium-sized whiting, or any suitable white fish
2 oz (50g) wholewheat flour, seasoned
2 lemons
2 oz (50g) butter
4 tablespoons chopped fennel

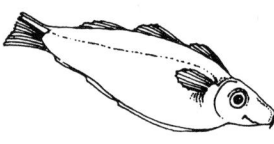

Clean the whiting and cut off the fins. The heads may be removed or left on. Coat the whiting in the seasoned flour. Cut one of the lemons into eight thin slices. Squeeze all the juice from the other lemon.

Melt half the butter in a large frying pan on a medium heat. Put in the whiting and fry them for about 4 minutes on each side, or until they are cooked through. If the pan is not big enough for all four, fry two at a time, adding a little more butter if needed.

Put the whiting on a warm serving plate and keep them warm. Put the lemon slices into the pan and brown them on both sides. Reserve them. Melt the remaining butter in the pan. Add the fennel and pour in the lemon juice. Let the mixture bubble and spoon it over the whiting. Top each fish with two of the lemon slices.

Serves 4

> Above the lower plants it towers,
> The Fennel with its yellow flowers;
> And in an earlier age than ours
> Was gifted with the wond'rous powers
> Lost vision to restore.
> It gave new strength and fearless mood;
> And gladiators, fierce and rude,
> Mingled it in their daily food;
> And he who battled and subdued,
> A wreath of fennel wore.
>
> LONGFELLOW

seeds were a substitute for juniper in the making of gin and today oil from the seeds flavours cordials and liqueurs.

— MEDICINAL USES —

Fennel tea is a mild carminative, relieving flatulence. It has diuretic properties and so is drunk by slimmers. It is also said to increase the milk flow of nursing mothers and to cure hiccoughs.

Infusions or decoctions of fennel were once used to bathe the eyes in order to strengthen them or cure cataract.

In Tudor Britain and also in China and India, fennel has been used to neutralize snake bites.

— SPECIAL USES —

Formerly fennel was a strewing herb used at weddings. The oil is an ingredient of soap and perfume and the dried leaves are suitable for potpourris and herb sachets.

Fennel will keep away fleas when placed among straw and bedding in kennels and stables.

— LORE —

Eating fennel is said to give longevity, strength and courage. From Roman until Tudor times it was a symbol of flattery.

In medieval Europe fennel was used to protect against witchcraft and was hung on the door on Midsummer's Eve to ward off evil spirits. It was also stuffed into the keyholes of bedchambers and hung on the rafters for the same purpose.

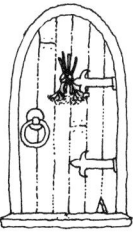

Fennel in potate and in mete
Is good to done whane yu shalt ete.
All grene looke it can be corwyn [carved] small
In what mete you usyn shall.

Fourteenth century manuscript

Sprinkle the chopped leaves over grilled or fried fish, add a sprig to baked fish or to a court bouillon for poaching, or include fennel in hot sauces and cold dressings.

Fennel also goes well with chicken and pork, so add it to stuffings and sauté dishes. A green summer salad will always benefit from a sprinkling of fennel leaves, and so will new carrots and white turnips. The blanched stems of fennel can be boiled like asparagus.

Add fennel to soups and savoury butters and use it as a flavouring for pickles and vinegars.

Roman bakers used to place sprigs of fennel under baking loaves and the ground seeds are now used to flavour bread and cakes. They can also be added to fruit pies.

In the eighteenth century, fennel

Garlic

A L L I U M   S A T I V U M

Garlic is an unusual herb in that it is not the leaves that are eaten but the bulbous, segmented corm. Since ancient times it has been both highly valued and looked upon with distaste. It flavours food, has great curative and preventative properties and has been attributed with the power of warding off evil; and yet there are many who have regarded it as a vulgar plant of little use but with an offensive smell.

Garlic has become so widely grown that its origin is obscure. It is thought to have come from either central Asia or western Siberia and is now naturalized all over the world.

One of the oldest of cultivated plants, garlic was revered by the ancient Hindus and Egyptians. It was eaten by workers building the Pyramids, both as a ritual and as a protection against illness. The Greeks and Romans consumed quantities of garlic and the second-century Greek physician Galen called it the peasants' *thereac*, or cure-all.

The Anglo-Saxons gave it its common name and in medieval Europe garlic was always to be found in herb gardens. In France it was macerated in wine or rubbed on bread to prevent drunkenness; English peasants and pilgrims chewed it to give them strength and resistance to disease. From the seventeenth century onwards, eating garlic was frowned upon in Britain but in Europe it retained a powerful attraction.

— CULTIVATION —

Plant the separate cloves of garlic in early spring in a soil previously enriched with manure or compost in the autumn. Plant them 2 inches (5cm) deep and 9 inches (22cm) apart in the rows, with the rows 12 inches (30cm) apart. Keep them well weeded. They will be ready to lift in late summer.

Dig up the garlic bulbs and spread them out to dry in the sun for an hour. Rub off the dirty outer skins and plait the bulbs together in bunches, about ten to a bunch. Store them in a cool

I have been spending some weeks of dissipation in London, and was transformed by Circe's cup, not into a brute, but a beau. I am now eating herb moly in the country.

SIDNEY SMITH, eighteenth century.

If everybody ate garlic, then nobody would find it objectionable.

French peasant

room or larder. The smell will disappear after the first week.

Planting garlic under peach trees is claimed as a cure for the disease known as leaf curl. Garlic is also said to increase the fragrance of roses when planted under the bushes.

— CULINARY USES —

Garlic is used worldwide. There are the famous dishes such as brandade, the gigot of lamb spiked with garlic and rosemary, seafood served with

aioli, and garlic soup. In addition, there are all the casseroles, sautés, stews and soups in which garlic is always present and which would never be so tasty if it were left out. For these, the garlic is usually chopped and first softened with onions before other ingredients are added.

Crushed raw garlic is added to salad dressings and sauces, to dips, soft cheeses and herb butters.

Boiled garlic has a much milder flavour and whole cloves can be treated in this way for making dips and pâtés and for adding to bread mixtures.

> The air of Provence is particularly perfumed by the refined essence of this mystically attractive bulb.
>
> ALEXANDRE DUMAS, nineteenth century

Garlic and Chickpea Dip

8 oz (225g) chickpeas, soaked and cooked
2 garlic bulbs (not cloves) boiled whole
for 20 minutes, drained
4 fl oz (125ml) olive oil
juice of 2 lemons
3 fl oz (90ml) tahini (sesame paste)
freshly ground black pepper
4 tablespoons chopped parsley
tomatoes for garnish

Put the chickpeas into a blender or food processor. Work them to a purée. Squeeze the garlic cloves from their skins and add them to the chickpeas. Put in the oil, lemon juice and tahini and blend again. Add the pepper and parsley and mix well.

Put the mixture into an oiled 30 fl oz (850ml) mould or tin and chill it for 2 hours. Turn it onto a plate and garnish with tomato wedges or slices.

Alternatively, the dip may be put into individual pots and not turned out. In this case garnish with either a small parsley sprig or half an olive.

Serves 6–8

— MEDICINAL USES —

Both the old practices and modern research have shown garlic to be a highly antiseptic internal purifier. Eating it regularly will build up a resistance to infection, aid digestion and help to keep down blood pressure. An infusion of crushed garlic relieves colds, coughs and whooping cough. Rub it on corns to soothe them, steep it in oil to ease sprains and rheumatic pains and apply it to wounds to prevent them from becoming septic.

In medieval times, garlic was recommended for leprosy and during the outbreak of fever in London in the nineteenth century it was proved by French priests to prevent infection.

However, it was disliked by many British physicians from the sixteenth century onwards. William Bullein in 1562 said it was a 'gross kind of medicine' very unpleasant for 'fayre Ladyes'.

For centuries garlic has been regarded as an antidote to drunkenness and overeating.

In the Mediterranean regions workers in the fields once rubbed cut garlic cloves on their lips and noses to prevent sunburn.

— LORE —

Garlic was worshipped by the Egyptians and also by Gypsies who called it 'moly'.

Greek herb gatherers had to smear themselves with large quantities of garlic before gathering roots. The Greeks also placed it on piles of stones at crossroads as a supper for Hecate, the goddess of the Underworld. However, those who had eaten garlic were forbidden to enter the temples of Cybele, the mother of the gods, because the scent was harmful to her magic.

The grandfather of the future Henri IV of France rubbed the newborn baby's lips with garlic and made him swallow a few drops of wine. This was to protect him from evil and to make sure that he could hold his drink.

In Eastern Europe, hanging garlic on the door or round your neck was said to deter vampires. In Sweden, the Trolls were the evil threat kept away by this practice.

Lemon Balm

M E L I S S A   O F F I C I N A L I S

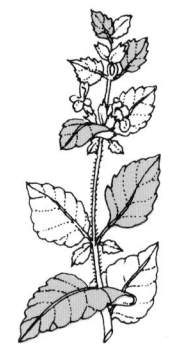

Lemon balm is a bushy plant with slightly hairy, heart-shaped leaves, whorls of tiny, cream-coloured flowers, and the sweet scent of lemon and honey. The old belief is that it makes a man merry and joyful. It is also well-loved by bees and *melissa*, the plant's botanical name, is the Greek word for bee. The name balm is the abbreviation of 'balsam', the most prized of sweet-smelling oils, given to this plant because of its sweetness.

The mountains of southern Europe were the original habitat of lemon balm, but now it is naturalized over much of the northern hemisphere, particularly on the sites of long-decayed buildings. It has always been a favourite plant in cottage gardens.

Lemon balm is a plant that has always been much praised. Both as a drink and used to make waters for washing, it was thought to ensure long life.

— CULTIVATION —

Lemon balm will grow well in any soil, but prefers to be in full sun where the ground is moist. It is best propagated by root division in spring or autumn. In spring, grow the divided plants on in a shady border and plant

Blackcurrant Mould

12 oz (350g) blackcurrants
3 tablespoons chopped lemon balm leaves
4 oz (125g) honey
½ oz (15g) gelatin
10 fl oz (275ml) thick cream
whole lemon balm leaves for garnish
candied angelica and glacé cherries, optional

String the blackcurrants. Put them into a saucepan with the chopped lemon balm leaves and honey. Cover them, and set them on a low heat for 15 minutes, or until they are very soft and juicy. Rub them through a sieve.

Return the purée to the cleaned pan. Set it on a low heat. Bring it almost to boiling point. Lightly sprinkle in the gelatin and stir until it has dissolved. Take the pan from the heat. Pour the jelly into a small pie dish or charlotte mould. Put it in the refrigerator for 3 hours to set.

Turn the mould on to a serving plate. Whip the cream and pipe it generously over the mould to cover it. Decorate with lemon balm leaves and add candied angelica and glacé cherries if required.

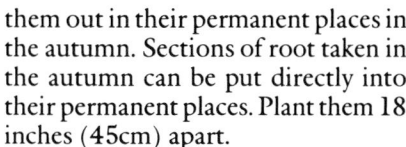

them out in their permanent places in the autumn. Sections of root taken in the autumn can be put directly into their permanent places. Plant them 18 inches (45cm) apart.

Harvest lemon balm just as it is coming into flower, since after flowering the scent is not so pleasant. Always cut the plants back in the autumn.

— CULINARY USES —

The chief use of lemon balm has always been to flavour and clarify wine and ale and in the Middle Ages it grew in every tavern garden. A sweet wine was made from the leaves, which were also used in preserves when lemons were scarce.

Add the leaves to wine cups and chilled summer drinks, or to a pot of China tea, or make a tisane with lemon balm only. Tart fruits gain a honey-like sweetness if lemon balm leaves are added to them while cooking. Milk for custards and sweet sauces can be gently heated with a sprig for a sweet lemon flavour.

Any savoury dish which would normally contain lemon rind or juice can also be flavoured with lemon balm. It is superb in stuffings for poultry, lamb and veal and also in sauté or braised dishes. Add it to fish dishes, to soups and to anything containing mushrooms.

Lay a pattern of leaves on the plate

The tender Leaves are us'd in Composition with other Herbs; and the Sprigs fresh gather'd, put into Wine or other Drinks, during the heat of Summer, give it a marvellous quickness: this noble Plant yields an incomparable wine.

JOHN EVELYN, *Acetaria*, 1699

before turning out pâtés or spooning on cream-cheese dips. Not only will they look attractive, they will also acquire a faint hint of lemon.

— MEDICINAL USES —

A tisane made from the leaves is soothing and reviving. Use it to help you relax and for various nervous complaints such as insomnia and headaches, and also to relieve menstrual pains. It is a palliative for feverish colds and influenza because of its cooling qualities.

— HOUSEHOLD USES —

Lemon balm was a favourite strewing herb as it disinfected as well as perfumed. The juice extracted from the stems and leaves was rubbed on furniture to make it shiny and sweet smelling. In Elizabethan times sprigs were used to make sweet-smelling chaplets and the leaves were put into baths.

The dried leaves give a fresh, sweet fragrance to pot-pourri and will also deter moths.

Lovage

LEVISTICUM OFFICINALE

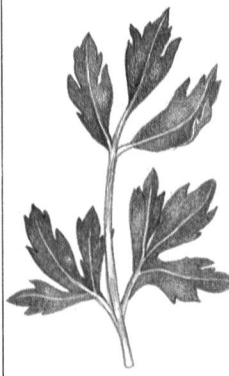

Lovage has been little used since the nineteenth century, but it should not be neglected since it is useful in both kitchen and bathroom and also as a medicinal plant. Every year lovage grows larger and after about four years it will grow to 6 feet (2 metres) or more. It is a robust, healthy-looking plant, with straight, hollow stems and large, shiny green leaves. Every part of it emits a strong, refreshing, celery-like aroma.

Lovage came from the Mediterranean area and it now grows wild in most of Europe, except in Britain, and in western Asia. There is another variety, known as Northern lovage or Scots parsley, which grows in Scotland and the English county of Northumberland, but its leaves are not so pleasant to taste. The Romans took lovage to Britain, and later it was grown in the monastery gardens of the Benedictine monks. It was popular as a pot herb in the Middle Ages and in 1557 Thomas Tusser listed it as one of the *Necessary Herbs to Grow in the Garden of Physic*. In the seventeenth century it was highly valued both in kitchen and still-room, but it fell from favour in the nineteenth century.

— CULTIVATION —

Lovage will grow well in any soil except heavy clay, but ideally its surroundings should be rich, moist and damp. It can be grown from seed but one plant will provide you with ample leaves all through the summer, and it is probably better to buy a single plant to propagate by root division in the spring or autumn. Simply take a small section of the root that has an 'eye' and plant it 2 inches

(5cm) deep in well-composted soil. Lovage plants should be set 3 feet (1 metre) apart.

Once your plants have become established, all you have to do is water them well during the summer and cut them back in early autumn. When harvesting, take off the leaves only, leaving the stalks undamaged. The root systems will grow larger each year and the plants become taller and bushier.

— CULINARY USES —

Because of its savoury, celery-like flavour, lovage has been for many years a favourite ingredient in soups, stews, broths and pottages and in Britain and Europe was regarded as a good substitute for pepper. Whenever you need the flavour of celery and none is available, a little lovage, either chopped or in a *bouquet garni*, will work just as well. Use it sparingly at first, for it is very strong. Lovage also makes a good addition to vegetarian dishes, taking the place of a yeast extract or vegetable stock cube. A sprig in the pot with boiling ham or bacon, or a poaching chicken, gives a delicious flavour.

White sauces for fish and some salad dressings can be flavoured with lovage. Chop the leaves into salads or rub a stem round the bowl before mixing a green salad. In New England, the leaves and stems are cooked as a vegetable.

In Italy, lovage seeds are put into bread, cakes and cheese biscuits. They are also added to casseroles of rabbit and hare.

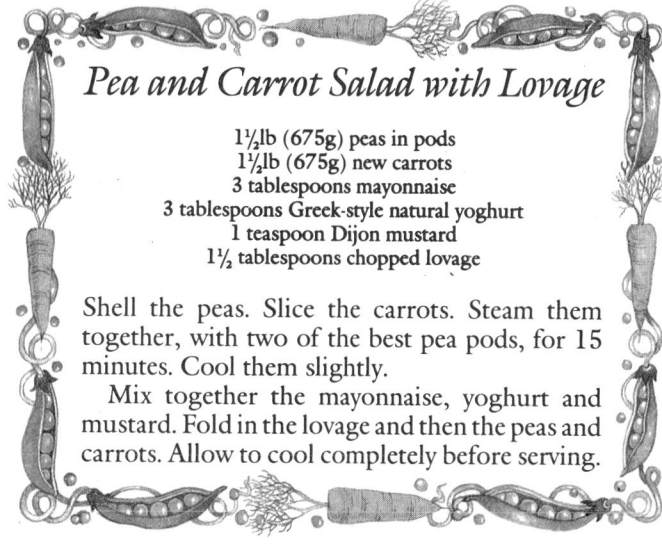

Pea and Carrot Salad with Lovage

1½lb (675g) peas in pods
1½lb (675g) new carrots
3 tablespoons mayonnaise
3 tablespoons Greek-style natural yoghurt
1 teaspoon Dijon mustard
1½ tablespoons chopped lovage

Shell the peas. Slice the carrots. Steam them together, with two of the best pea pods, for 15 minutes. Cool them slightly.

Mix together the mayonnaise, yoghurt and mustard. Fold in the lovage and then the peas and carrots. Allow to cool completely before serving.

— MEDICINAL USES —

Hot lovage tea, which in fact tastes more like a broth, is soothing and relaxing. It makes a good gargle for a sore throat and, taken every day, is said to ease rheumatism, stimulate the kidneys and sweeten the breath. In India it is used to treat cholera.

A decoction or infusion of lovage is mildly antiseptic and used externally will aid in the healing of wounds and ulcers. It has also been tried as a way of removing spots and freckles from the face.

— LORE —

Lovage has been used as an aphrodisiac and as a love charm. Czechoslovakian girls had a custom of hanging a bag of lovage around the neck when going to meet a sweetheart.

Lovage leaves or a decoction of lovage added to the bath act as a fresh scented deodorant. A lovage bath is refreshing and relaxing.

The distilled water of Lovage cleareth the sight and putteth away all spots, lentils, freckles and redness of the face, if they be often washed therewith.

JOHN GERARD, 1597

Marigold

C A L E N D U L A   O F F I C I N A L I S

The sweet, humble marigold is now looked on as simply a cottage garden plant, but it has been a valued pot-herb and is still used medicinally.

The marigold is a native of southern Europe where it grows wild in vineyards and fields. It was not used by the Romans but was well known to the Saxons. It was taken to South America by the Spaniards and to North America by the early settlers. Its oldest name is 'ymbglidegold' meaning 'that which moves round the sun', since during the day its flowers turn to follow the sun and then close up at night. In later years it was associated with the Virgin Mary and also with Queen Mary Tudor of England. It is said to bloom in the calends of every month, the first day of the month in the Roman calendar, hence its Latin name *Calendula*.

The marigold has always been much loved because of its long flowering season, its many culinary and medicinal uses and because it is a pretty, friendly, and unassuming plant.

— CULTIVATION —

Marigolds are easy to grow and, although annual plants, may flower throughout the year where the weather is mild. Sow the seeds in spring in a sunny spot and keep them well weeded. The first flowers should appear in late spring or early summer and, if you cut back all the dead heads, you should get another show in early autumn. Cut them back again and the sturdiest plants will last through the winter to flower once more in late spring. If you allow some of the summer flowers to seed, there will be no need to sow again in the following spring. If a marigold patch is left unattended, it will spread rapidly.

— CULINARY USES —

Marigold petals, added to soups, casseroles and stews and stuffings, impart a mild, warming flavour and a slight colour. They may also be added to sweet puddings and cakes and used to colour cheese and butter. Mix them with chives into cream or cottage cheese for both flavour and attractive appearance. The bright petals make a pretty addition to rice dishes, hot and cold, sweet and savoury, and also to salads. There has also been a traditional practice of picking the flowers and making them into wines and cordials.

— MEDICINAL USES —

An infusion of marigold flowers is soothing and relaxing. Drunk hot it helps the body to sweat out a fever, and taken regularly is said to ease varicose veins. It can be used as a mild eye-bath for tired eyes and as a rub to ease the pain of bee and wasp stings.

A decoction of the flowers can be drunk in cases of smallpox and

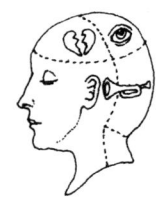

measles; or made into a compress for sprains and rheumatic pains, burns and bruises.

The flowers can be made into a compress for relief of chilblains or, for the same purpose, a decoction can be added to a foot bath. Marigold leaves wrapped around clean, shallow cuts and scratches quickly stop the bleeding.

The wound-healing properties of the marigold have long been known and the plant was much used by both sides during the American Civil War.

As *Calendula*, marigolds are used in homeopathic ointments and tinctures.

Courgette and Cheese Ramekins with Marigold Petals

12 oz (350g) small courgettes (zucchini)
4 oz (125g) Cheddar cheese, grated
1 oz (25g) butter
2 tablespoons chopped parsley
petals from 6 marigold flowers

Wipe the courgettes and coarsely grate them. Dice the cheese finely. Melt the butter in a saucepan on a moderate heat. Fold in the courgettes and cook them, stirring, for 2 minutes. Mix in the parsley. Fold in the cheese and let it heat through without melting. Mix in the petals from four marigold flowers.

Take the pan from the heat immediately and put the courgettes into four small dishes. Scatter the remaining marigold petals over the top.

Serves 4 as a first course

— SPECIAL USES —

Decoctions of marigold flowers were once used as a yellow hair dye. In the English Tudor courts, ladies wore wreaths of marigolds and heartsease in their hair.

Dried marigold flowers add colour, but not scent, to pot-pourri.

— LORE —

Marigold has been a symbol of constancy, as it never turns its face from the sun. It has also been a symbol of endurance. In association with heartsease, it means 'happiness stored in recollections' in the language of flowers. In southern Europe girls took earth from a lover's footprint, put it in a pot and planted a marigold in it.

In the Middle Ages, however, marigolds symbolized jealousy. Chaucer wrote of Jealousy wearing a garland of Marigolds. In the old carol, *Lord Jesus Hath a Garden*, it stood for obedience.

In Mexico the marigold was the flower of death, and was believed to have sprung from the blood of the natives killed by Spanish invaders.

The yellow leaves of the flowers are dried and kept throughout Dutchland against winter to put into broths, physicall potions and for divers other purposes, in such quantity that in some Grocers or Spicesellers are to be found barrells filled with them and retailed by three penny or less, insomuch that no broths are well made without dried Marigolds.

JOHN GERARD, 1597

Marjoram

O R I G A N U M   V U L G A R E

Sweetly-scented marjoram is a native of the Mediterranean regions, but it now grows wild throughout Europe, Asia and North Africa, in England and Ireland and in the United States, particularly in the Catskill Mountains.

Marjoram was used medicinally by the ancient Greeks and in medieval times was grown in monastery herbariums. In England it was popular in Tudor and Stuart knot gardens, and in the eighteenth century was one of the 'sweet herbs' used with meats. Until the early nineteen-thirties marjoram tea was frequently drunk in the homes of country people in England, but as a kitchen herb marjoram has only been popular in American kitchens over the last thirty years.

There are many different types of marjoram. *Origanum vulgare*, also called wild marjoram, oregano and Joy of the Mountain is an easy-to-grow perennial and is therefore the type most commonly seen in herb gardens. It has a very sweet scent and is a bushy plant with mauve flowers, growing to about 9 inches (22cm) in height. Sweet or Knotted marjoram, *Origanum marjorana*, has a spicy, sweet scent and small white flowers; it should be grown as an annual in cooler climates. Pot marjoram, *Origanum onites*, is a dainty, low growing plant with a stronger flavour than *Origanum vulgare*. It is a perennial which dies down in winter and its leaves are either deep green or variegated. There is also Winter marjoram, *Origanum heraclioticum*, with a flavour similiar to the wild marjoram, but milder, and various other types of marjoram that are suitable for rock gardens.

And the sweet Marjoram with your garden paint
With no gay colours, yet preserve the plant,
Whose fragrance will invite your kind regard,
When her known virtues have her worth declared!
On Simor's shore fair Venus raised the plant,
Which from the Goddess' touch derived her scent.

RENÉ RAPIN

All types of marjoram love a sunny situation and a light, dry soil. They can be grown from seed in spring in drills 9 inches (22cm) apart. When they are 1 inch (2.5cm) high, thin the plants to 8 inches (20cm) apart.

The perennial marjorams can be propagated by root division in the autumn or by taking cuttings, each with a 'heel', in midsummer. These should be established in pots before planting out in the autumn. Keep all varieties well weeded and cut the perennials back to the new growth in autumn.

— CULINARY USES —

Although marjoram is one of the so called 'sweet herbs', it is used extensively in savoury dishes. It was one of the favourite culinary herbs of the eighteenth century, when cooks were discovering the delights of subtle flavourings rather than strong mixtures of spices. Its mild antiseptic properties also helped to prevent bad flavours in meat that had been kept for some time.

With parsley, thyme and bay, marjoram is an essential part of a *bouquet garni*. Add it to sausages and to stuffings for pork, lamb, veal and poultry. Chop it and use it in beef casseroles, stews and sauté dishes and also in vegetarian bean and nut dishes, and with pasta. Root vegetables benefit from a sprinkling of marjoram and it goes exceptionally well with tomatoes. In Spain it is added to lettuce salad. If you are adding chopped marjoram to any dish, use the leaves only and discard the woody stems.

Infuse marjoram in milk to prevent it going sour in thundery weather. The herb also gives milk a sweet flavour, for drinking and suitable for making milk puddings. Marjoram tea was a popular country drink and the herb was also used to flavour beer and ale. A conserve of marjoram was made in the eighteenth century and it was used to flavour a sweet cordial drink or sherbet originating from the Middle East, known as Sikenjebin.

Skirt of Beef with Sweet Herbs

2 lb (900g) skirt of beef
1 oz (25g) butter
2 medium onions, thinly sliced
15 fl oz (425 ml) stock
2 tablespoons chopped marjoram
2 tablespoons chopped parsley
1 tablespoon chopped lemon thyme, or common thyme
4 sage leaves, chopped
4 anchovy fillets, finely chopped
grated rind of a lemon

Cut the beef into 1 inch (2.5cm) cubes. Heat the butter in a large sauté pan or frying pan on a high heat. Put in the beef and brown it well. Remove it and lower the heat. Mix in the onions and cook them until they are soft and golden. Pour in the stock and bring it to the boil. Mix in the herbs, anchovy fillets and lemon rind. Replace the beef. Cover and cook on a very low heat for 1 hour.

Serves 4

A CONSERVE OF MARJORAM

Take the tops and tenderest parts of Sweet Marjoram, bruise it well in a wooden Mortar or Bowl; take double the weight of Fine Sugar, boil it with Marjoram Water till it is as thick as Syrup, then put in your beaten Majoram.

From the Receipt Book of John Nott, cook to the Duke of Bolton, 1723

— MEDICINAL USES —

Wild marjoram and sweet marjoram are the types used medicinally and their properties are similar. They have been valued for this purpose since the days of the ancient Greeks who used marjoram against narcotic poisoning and dropsy. Marjoram tea was considered to be a tonic in Britain until quite recently. Even the scent of marjoram was once thought to maintain good health.

An infusion of marjoram is an aid to digestion which also sweetens the breath and helps to expel poisons from the body. It is very calming and can be of benefit to anyone suffering symptoms of nervous origin such as headache, depression, nightmares or unfounded fears. It is also recommended for seasickness. According to Gerard it 'easeth such as are given to overmuch sighing'.

Sniffing the fresh leaves or taking the dried leaves as snuff relieves a stuffy nose. An infusion gargled or drunk helps a sore throat, as does a cloth soaked in a warm decoction and wrapped around the neck. This compress will also ease earache and a stiff neck. Add the decoction to a warm bath to soak away tension and macerate the herb in oil as a rub for muscular, nervous and rheumatic pains.

A clergyman running an asylum for orphans once claimed marjoram tea to be 'a most useful sexual nerve sedative'.

— HOUSEHOLD USES —

Marjoram was a strewing herb, used also for making sweet bags and pot-pourri and sweet washing waters for the table. It was rubbed over wooden furniture to clean it and give a spicy scent.

The flowers can be used to dye wool a purple colour and linen a red-brown.

— LORE —

A Roman story told that marjoram was first raised by Venus; because of this it was made into wreaths to crown the bride and groom at weddings.

Another story concerns a youth in the service of King Cinyras of Cyprus. Carrying a jar of precious perfumes, he stumbled and dropped it, and was so frightened of the King's anger that he lost consciousness and turned into wild marjoram.

The Greeks planted marjoram on graves in order to help the dead sleep happily.

With Marjerain gentle
The flower of goodly head
Embroidered the mantle
Is of your maidenhead.

SKELTON, *To Maistress Margary Wentworth*

Goats and sheep are fond of marjoram and it will give a sweet taste to their milk.

 # Mint

M E N T H A S P I C A T A

Refreshing, cooling mint came originally from the Mediterranean and it travelled first with the Romans and later with other explorers and settlers to most countries of the world, where it is now both cultivated and naturalized.

The many varieties have been valued medicinally since ancient times. Greeks and Romans crowned themselves with peppermint at their feasts and put bunches on the tables. Mints were mentioned in herbals written in the ninth and thirteenth centuries and were cultivated in monastery and convent gardens in Saxon times. The Pilgrim Fathers took them to America where they quickly became naturalized and were cultivated on a large scale. Michigan and Ohio are still important producers of peppermint. Large amounts of mint were also cultivated in south-east England until the nineteen-thirties.

In 1597, John Gerard recorded that 'there be divers sorts of Mints, some of the garden, others wilde or of the field; and also some of water', and several different types are still cultivated today. Spearmint, *Mentha spicata*, is the one most associated with the kitchen although Apple mint, *Mentha rotundifolia*, once known as the monk's herb, has a sweeter flavour and is preferred by many cooks. Peppermint, *Mentha piperata*, with its purple-tinged leaves, is grown for tea and for its oil.

Winter mint, *Mentha cordifolia*, has a similar flavour to spearmint and has the advantage of not dying back in the winter. Pineapple mint, *Mentha rotundifolia variegata*, is most often grown as a decorative aromatic plant, although it can be used for tea and fruit desserts. Eau de Cologne mint, *Mentha citrata*, is mainly regarded as aromatic but it can also be used in the kitchen. Corn mint, *Mentha arvensis*, and Water mint, *Mentha aquatica*, may be found growing wild and can be used like spearmint.

— CULTIVATION —

Mints will grow in almost any soil. They like to be in full sun but need to be watered in the summer to prevent them from becoming straggly. Cut the plants back after they have flowered to encourage them to grow bushy.

Mints are best propagated by dividing the roots in the autumn. Dig up the tangle of roots and break them into pieces about 3 inches (7.5cm) long. Plant them about 3 inches (7.5cm) deep in well-composted soil.

Minted Aubergines

2 large aubergines (eggplants)
1 tablespoon sea salt
juice of one lemon
4 tablespoons chopped mint
1 teaspoon ground cumin
1 garlic clove, crushed
freshly ground black pepper

For the sauce:
5 fl oz (150ml) natural yoghurt
4 tablespoons chopped mint
½ teaspoon ground cumin

Cut the aubergines into ⅜ inch (1cm) thick slices and layer them in a colander with the salt. Leave them to drain for 30 minutes. Wash them under cold water and dry them on kitchen paper. Beat together the oil, lemon juice, mint, cumin, garlic and pepper. Beat together the ingredients for the sauce.

Heat the grill to high. Lay the aubergine slices on the hot rack and brush them with half the lemon mixture. Grill them until they are beginning to brown, about 2 minutes. Turn them over and brush them with the remaining dressing. Brown the second side.

Serve hot, with the sauce separately, as a starter; or on a large serving plate, with the sauce spooned over the aubergines, as an accompaniment for lamb and middle-eastern dishes.

Serves 4

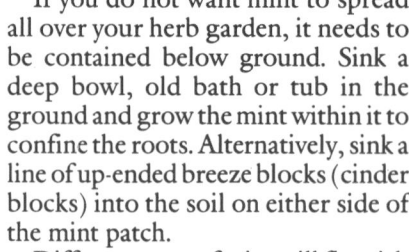

If you do not want mint to spread all over your herb garden, it needs to be contained below ground. Sink a deep bowl, old bath or tub in the ground and grow the mint within it to confine the roots. Alternatively, sink a line of up-ended breeze blocks (cinder blocks) into the soil on either side of the mint patch.

Different types of mint will flourish side by side, although sometimes they may hybridize.

— CULINARY USES —

In the kitchen, mint has been most popular in the Middle East and in Britain. The Greeks and Romans used it as a relish for meat and both Britain and the Arab countries use it with lamb, in Britain as a sauce made with vinegar or as a sweet mint jelly, and in the Middle East in sauces and chutneys and sprinkled over spicy dishes such as couscous.

Mint enhances summer vegetables. Add a sprig to new carrots, green peas, broad beans or new potatoes, or toss them with mint and melted butter after cooking.

Apple mint, eau de Cologne mint and pineapple mint give a fresh flavour to summer fruit salads and other cold desserts. Mint pasty, with a filling of chopped mint, brown sugar and currants, is a speciality of the north of England.

Many drinks have been flavoured with mint. Peppermint makes a refreshing tea that can be drunk hot or cold, simply for pleasure or as an aid to digestion. Commercially, spearmint is used to flavour Crème de

Menthe, Chartreuse and Benedictine. Mint Julep is a cocktail based on Bourbon whisky popular in the United States. The Greeks and Romans scented their wine with mint and in the Middle East the chilled yoghurt drink known as ayran is often served with a sprinkling of chopped mint. Add mint sprigs to summer punches and cups or infuse them in apple juice or milk. In earlier times, sprigs of mint were put into milk to prevent it from curdling.

Oil of peppermint flavours many different sweets and confections.

— MEDICINAL USES —

All mints are refreshing and reviving made into tea or added to fruit cups.

They are highly digestive, particularly peppermint, and will ease upset stomachs and relieve hiccoughs and nausea. Mint should not, however, be drunk by pregnant or nursing mothers as it can inhibit the supply of milk.

Peppermint tea induces mild perspiration so it is good for colds and influenza, especially when made with a mixture of peppermint, yarrow and elderflowers.

Old herbalists recommended rubbing bee and wasp stings with mint leaves. A decoction was put into the bath 'as a help to comfort and strengthen the nerves and sinews'. Made strong, it was rubbed on chapped hands. Mints of various kinds were an important ingredient in many early tooth-cleaning preparations and peppermint water was used as a face lotion and was put into smelling-bottles to prevent swooning.

— SPECIAL USES —

Spearmint is loved by bees and it was once the custom to rub it on the inside of hives. Mice and rats hate the scent of peppermint, so plants were grown near food crops to keep rodents at bay, and rags soaked in the oil were used to block up mouse-holes.

Mints were a strewing herb in Roman times and also later in England where they were popular for church pews and great halls. Most kinds can be used in pot-pourri.

Roman matrons made a paste of mint and honey to disguise the fact that they had been drinking wine. Had they been found out, the punishment would have been death, since wine was only for men and the gods.

— LORE —

In ancient mythology, Menthe was a nymph loved by Pluto who was turned into mint by Proserpine, Pluto's jealous wife.

In France and Spain mint was for a long time regarded as one of the sacred herbs.

There was an old belief that mint should never be cut with iron. Nicholas Culpeper quoted the superstition that if a wounded man eats mint he will never recover.

 # Parsley

PETROSELINUM SATIVUM

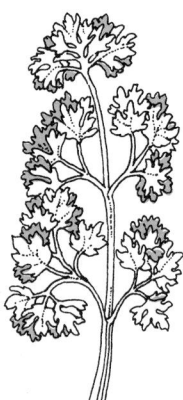

Parsley is a well-known and much used herb and yet its precise origin is unknown. It is probably from Sardinia and other parts of southern Europe. Its name comes from the Greek *petro* meaning rock or stone, because it could be found in stony places. This became corrupted in the Middle Ages to petersylinge, and then through pesele and persely, eventually to become parsley.

It was used by the Greeks and Romans, grown in the herb gardens of the Emperor Charlemagne in the eighth century, was well known in England in medieval times and taken to America by the early settlers.

There are many different types of parsley, but the best known are the moss-curled type and French parsley which has broad, flat leaves.

— CULTIVATION —

Parsley is slow to germinate and there are many superstitions built upon this fact. It goes nine, or sometimes seven, times to the devil and back again before it appears above the soil, was one popular belief.

When it comes to flowering, parsley is a biennial, but spring-sown seed will produce plenty of usable leaves by early summer. Sow in warm moist soil in late winter for early leaves and again in mid spring for harvesting from late summer into winter. Seed sown in midsummer will be ready for cutting late in the following winter. Sow in drills 8 inches (20cm) apart and thin to 8 inches (20cm) apart when the seedlings are 1 inch (2.5cm) high. Water them well in dry weather.

The following year, old plants will flower early, but if the flowerheads are removed as soon as they appear, you will still get a supply of usable leaves.

— CULINARY USES —

Where would the cook be without parsley? It is an essential part of a *bouquet garni* and goes well with all meats and poultry. Add chopped parsley to casseroles and sauté dishes and also to stuffings and sauces. Put in a sprig when poaching, boiling or pot-roasting or scatter it over the top of the finished dish as a garnish. Toss cooked vegetables in parsley and butter and add parsley to dishes of pulses and nuts. Omelettes, soufflés, quiches and roulades and even egg mayonnaise all benefit from the addition of parsley.

Henry VIII of England loved parsley and one of his favourite dishes was roasted rabbit with parsley sauce. The Emperor Charlemagne yearly ate three cases of parsley cheese and earlier still, Pliny recommended it as a pottage herb, a use to which it was well put in the Middle Ages.

If you are served a dish garnished with parsley, always eat the garnish

... parsley is in great request ... and no man lightly there is but loveth it: for nothing is there more ordinary than to see large branches of parsley good store, swimming in their pottage.

PLINY

for parsley is rich in vitamins A, B and C plus iron, calcium, magnesium and other important trace elements.

— MEDICINAL USES —

For many years eating parsley or drinking parsley tea has been known to have a beneficial effect on the kidneys. Parsley tea was used in the trenches in World War I to cure kidney problems brought on by dysentery. It also stimulates the whole of the digestive system.

Asparagus and Parsley Quiche

shortcrust pastry made with 8 oz (225g) wholewheat flour
¹⁄₂lb (675g) asparagus
¹⁄₂oz (40g) parsley, finely chopped
4 eggs
8oz (225g) curd cheese

Heat the oven to 400°F/200°C/gas mark 6. Trim the tough ends from the asparagus. Steam or boil the tips until they are tender. Reserve six tips and finely chop the rest.

Beat the eggs. Put the cheese into a bowl and gradually beat in the eggs to make a smooth, creamy mixture. Mix in the chopped asparagus and parsley.

Roll out the pastry and use it to line a 10 inch (25cm) tart tin. Put in the egg mixture. Gently roll the reserved tips in the mixture and then arrange them in a radiating pattern in the centre.

Bake the quiche for 30 minutes or until the top is set but not coloured. Serve warm or cold.

Serves 6

An old remedy for rheumatism was to drink parsley tea; parsley simmered in wine was made into a poultice for sprains. A wad of cotton wool soaked in a decoction of parsley is said to ease both earache and toothache.

As a soothing remedy for tired or sore eyes, lie down and put a dressing of crushed parsley on your closed eyelids. Rubbing on the crushed leaves also eases insect bites and a strong infusion massaged into the scalp has been used to clear headlice. Parsley seeds sprinkled into the hair were thought to be a cure for baldness.

— SPECIAL USES —

The Chinese name for parsley is translated as 'kill-flea'; in the west of Ireland parsley was strewn under the beds to rid the rooms of fleas.

Parsley is beneficial to animals as well as humans. Given regularly to sheep, parsley is supposed to help to prevent foot rot. Greek warriors fed parsley to their chariot horses.

— LORE —

Good Friday was traditionally the chosen day for sowing parsley. This would ensure that the devil would not get it and that it would bring good luck. Always sow it along a garden, for it is unlucky to sow it across.

It is said that it takes an honest man to grow parsley well and also that if the mistress sows the parsley, it always flourishes and so will she. Where the parsley thrives 'the missus is master' goes a saying from Devon. Another is that if your parsley thrives your daughter will be a spinster.

Parsley be also delightful to the taste, and agreeable to the stomacke.

JOHN GERARD, 1597

In many countries it is considered unlucky to transplant parsley and also to give it away. '*Repiquer le persil, repiquer sa femme*' (Plant out parsley, plant out your wife) is said in France. Negroes in the southern states of America believed it was unlucky to take parsley from the old house to the new, and in Cornwall it was unlucky to give away parsley leaves, although they could be sold. In the Middle Ages it was thought that a man was condemned to death if his name was uttered while pulling up parsley.

The Romans wore parsley leaves around their necks to prevent drunkenness and in sixteenth-century England the seeds were chewed for the same reason. The seeds were also thought to increase fertility in both men and women.

The saying 'We are at the parsley and rue' means we are at the beginning of a project, for the Greeks bordered their herb gardens with the plants.

In Greek mythology, parsley was said to have sprung from the blood of the hero Archemorus as the forerunner of death, so it was one of the sacred burial herbs. The Greeks also crowned their champions with parsley wreaths at the Isthmian games.

In early Christian times, parsley was dedicated to Saint Peter.

If you will have the leaves of parcelye grow crisped, then before the sowing of them stuffe a tennis ball with the seedes and beat the same well against the ground whereby the seeds may be a little bruised or when the percelye is well come up go over the bed with a waighty roller whereby it may so presse the leaves down.

The Grete Herball, 1539

Rosemary

ROSMARINUS OFFICINALIS

The beautiful, aromatic rosemary, with its spiky leaves and shy blue flowers takes its name from Latin words meaning 'dew of the sea', for rosemary grows wild on Mediterranean coasts where its grey-bloomed leaves make the hillsides look as though they are covered in dew. In later years its name and its many healing properties led it to be associated with the Virgin Mary.

Romans carried rosemary to other parts of Europe and to Britain where it is said to grow better than anywhere else, as the damp climate gives it a delicate fragrance. Rosemary was mentioned in an Anglo-Saxon herbal, *The Leech Book of Bald*, in the tenth century, but the court of Edward III of England in the fourteenth century appears not to have taken notice of it until Queen Philippa was sent some plants by her mother, the Countess of Hainault, together with a long manuscript describing its many virtues.

From then on, rosemary became one of the most popular herbs and it certainly had many medicinal, culinary and aromatic uses. It was loved most of all by the people of Tudor England, who grew it in pots and against walls and used it in topiary. In 1597 John Gerard recorded that it could even be found growing wild in Lancashire. Later, rosemary was taken to America by early settlers.

There are basically three types of rosemary; that which will grow into a bush in a herb garden or pot, one that is best grown up walls and a prostrate variety that will cover banks or the tops of walls.

— CULTIVATION —

Rosemary likes a warm, sheltered spot, preferably against a wall receiving midday or afternoon sun. It flourishes best in a well-drained, sandy soil given an occasional dressing of lime or crushed eggshells. No composting is necessary.

Rosemary can be grown from seed, which should be started off in pots or trays indoors on a sunny windowsill. When the seedlings are about 1½ inches (4cm) high, transfer them to individual pots of sandy soil and keep them under glass for the first winter, planting them out in late spring or

As for Rosemarine, I lett it runne all over my garden walls, not onlie because my bees love it, but because it is the herb sacred to remembrance, and, therefore, to friendship.

SIR THOMAS MORE

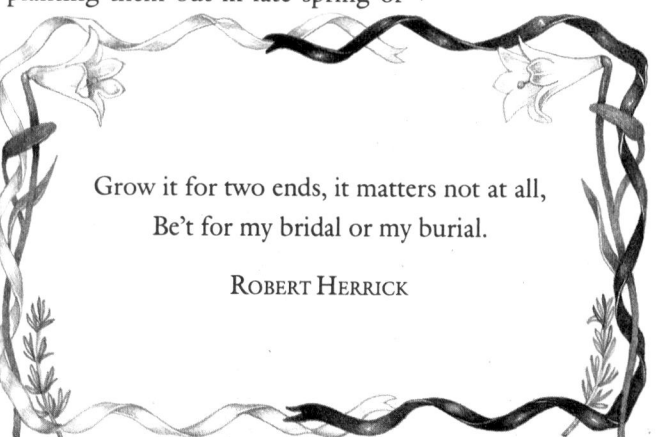

Grow it for two ends, it matters not at all,
Be't for my bridal or my burial.

ROBERT HERRICK

early summer of the following year. You can also propagate rosemary from cuttings taken at this time of year. Take them with a 'heel', dip them in rooting powder and set them in pots of sandy soil. They can be planted out in the autumn but must be protected by a sheet of polythene for the first winter. In fact, if you live in an area that is subject to harsh winters, all rosemary plants should be protected in this way.

In order to prevent it from becoming straggly, rosemary should be trimmed into shape every autumn. Constant cutting of the tips throughout spring and summer will encourage it to grow bushy.

— CULINARY USES —

Rosemary is most often associated with lamb, but pork, beef and poultry all benefit from a hint of rosemary. Cut slits in lamb or pork and insert rosemary leaves before roasting. This would be too much for beef or poultry, so simply lay a few sprigs over a roasting joint or add them to a marinade. You can also add chopped rosemary leaves to stuffings and herb butters but do so sparingly at first, for they can be very pungent. Add a few of the tenderest leaves from the tips of the plant to a salad, or steep a sprig in wine vinegar for dressing a salad.

Rosemary also goes well with fruit. Add it to jellies for serving with meats, add a sprig to poached fruits or boil it in the syrup for a fruit salad. Sprigs of rosemary steeped in honey give it an aromatic flavour.

Country housewives would always

make their own lard at pig-killing time and the fat for this was often rendered with a sprig of rosemary which gave its flavour to the bread, cakes and biscuits for which the lard was later used. The chopped leaves can be added in the same way to bread, biscuits and shortbreads.

When making a drink of mixed

Pot-Roasted Neck of Lamb with Rosemary

2lb (900g) neck of lamb
1 garlic clove
1 tablespoon olive oil
5 fl oz (150ml) stock
2 teaspoons chopped rosemary
2 tablespoons red wine vinegar
sea salt and freshly ground black pepper

Heat the oven to 350°F/180°C/gas mark 4. Chop the lamb into small pieces and remove any excess fat. Make slits in the lamb pieces and insert thin slivers of garlic. Lightly oil a flameproof casserole and set it on a high heat. Put in the pieces of lamb, brown them and remove them. Do this in two batches if necessary. Pour away all the fat from the casserole.

Set the casserole back on the stove. Pour in the stock and bring it to the boil. Add the rosemary and vinegar and season lightly. Replace the lamb. Cover the casserole and put it into the oven for 1 hour 30 minutes.

Serves 4

fruit juices, infuse a sprig of rosemary in it for a while before serving. Rosemary has also been used to flavour wine and ale, mead, cordial drinks and hot possets. The flowers were candied and the leaves used to flavour conserves.

— MEDICINAL USES —

Rosemary has been one of the most used of medicinal herbs, valued by the Greeks and Romans and throughout history to the present day.

The Romans put rosemary into their baths to ease tired and aching limbs. A rosemary bath both soothes and refreshes.

Since early times infusions of rosemary and wine flavoured with rosemary have been drunk for their calming effect on the nerves. Nervous headaches, tremblings and other such complaints have been treated in this way. Rosemary tea is also a well-known breath sweetener.

The antiseptic properties of rosemary are well known; it was carried in churches, court rooms and other public places in times of plague and until the beginning of the present century was burnt with juniper berries in hospitals and sickrooms to fumigate the air. In Spain it is pounded with salt as a cure for wounds and in Arab countries dried powdered leaves are sprinkled on the umbilical cords of infants.

Rosemary drunk as an infusion stimulates the circulation and helps low blood pressure. Oil of rosemary rubbed on the chest eases a cough, as do the dried leaves taken as snuff.

A decoction of rosemary used as a rinse will condition the hair and stimulate growth. Olive oil in which rosemary has been steeped can be used as a conditioner for dry hair.

— HOUSEHOLD USES —

Laid amongst clothes, sprigs of rosemary are a good moth deterrent. It has been used in the making of eau de Cologne and other toilet and sweet washing waters, as well as mixtures to beautify the complexion.

The wood was once used to make lutes and other musical instruments.

— LORE —

Rosemary is the herb of remembrance. Greek scholars wore it on their heads to help them retain information and it was used to decorate churches at funerals. Rosemary has been carried at weddings to represent the fidelity of lovers and gilded sprigs were exchanged as tokens between friends. In medieval and Tudor times in England, it was one of the evergreens which decorated houses and churches at Christmas and the traditional roasted boar's head always had a rosemary garland.

Rosemary was thought to keep away evil spirits and a sprig was laid under the pillow to prevent nightmares.

There is a legend that rosemary flowers are blue because it was one of the bushes that sheltered the Holy family on the flight into Egypt. Mary laid her cloak over the white flowers on the bushes and they have been blue ever since.

Make thee a box of the wood of rosemary and smell to it and it shall preserve thy youth.

From the manuscript of the Countess of Hainault, quoted in *Bankes' Herbal*, 1525

It is an holy tree and with ffolke that been just and Rightfulle gladlye it groweth and thriveth.

ibid.

Sage

SALVIA OFFICINALIS

Throughout the world, there are many different varieties of sage, from the highly decorative garden plants with variegated leaves, to the wild varieties that grow in the Spanish hills, along the coasts of the Mediterranean and the Adriatic, and in the Rocky Mountains.

Sage was growing wild in southern Europe in Roman times. Roman soldiers took it north to France, Germany and Britain. In medieval times, sage was the most popular of culinary and medicinal herbs, and is still one of the most commonly used herbs for cooking.

— CULTIVATION —

Sage grows well in any type of soil, although it prefers a warm, dry spot. Slight shade is beneficial, but sage does not flourish under trees.

Sage is a hardy perennial and plants will last for years. However, after about four years the plants tend to become woody and 'leggy', so it is best to take cuttings at about this time. After a rainy day in early autumn, cut off suitable twigs and simply stick them in the ground. Put a little compost around them and they should take root quickly.

Always cut mature plants right back in early autumn to ensure vigorous growth the following spring.

— CULINARY USES —

All varieties of sage can be used in the kitchen. Many cooks prefer the narrow-leaved white sage, and that is the one most commonly found in English and American gardens. Others say that the red sage, *Salvia officinalis purpurea*, has the finer flavour, while those who can obtain the wild variety may find that it surpasses all others for its strong, spicy flavour.

Since early times, sage has been thought to aid in the digestion of rich meats, so it has been used mainly with pork, duck and goose, and also with eel and other oily fish.

From English kitchens have come countless recipes for sage and onion stuffing or sauces, and sage forcemeat balls. Many sausages are flavoured with sage and faggots, too, have been made extra tasty with this herb.

In Italy, veal rather than pork is thought to benefit from the flavour of

Between Gosport and Southampton we observed a little Churchyard where it was customary to sow all graves with sage.

SAMUEL PEPYS, seventeenth century

In short, 'tis a plant endu'ud with so many and wonderful properties that the assiduous use of it is said to render Men immortal.

JOHN EVELYN, 1699

In the Jura area of France, sage is said to ease grief. In seventeenth century England, sage was planted on graves for the same reason.

sage, in dishes such as piccate, saltimbocca and ossi buchi. In the Middle East, where pork is forbidden, sage is threaded onto kebabs between the cubes of lamb. German cooks add it to tripe, spit-roasted ham and eels. In Eastern Europe, sage is mixed with marjoram and paprika as a flavouring for liver and kidneys.

With its strong flavour, sage may not be everyone's choice for a salad herb, but if it is used sparingly it goes exceptionally well with cooling summer salads of lettuce, cucumber and spring onions.

Sage is excellent with cheese, in cooked dishes. It can also be used to flavour the cheese itself, as in the Sage Derby cheese made in England and the Vermont Sage cheese of the USA. Chopped sage may also be added to curd or cottage cheese.

Sage tea is a pleasant and refreshing drink, particularly when flavoured with honey and a squeeze of lemon juice. Sage steeped in apple juice lends an interesting flavour. A Dutch drink, traditionally served after skating, is hot milk flavoured with sage.

— MEDICINAL USES —

Sage has always been a highly acclaimed medicinal plant. 'Why should a man die when sage grows in his garden?' is a saying that has been quoted since medieval times. Red sage and broad-leaved white sage are the ones most used medicinally.

In many countries sage has been used as a spring tonic and blood cleanser, taken in the form of sage tea, or in sandwiches. An infusion or

Sage and Onion Stuffing

2 large onions
10 fl oz (275ml) milk
2 bay leaves
8 oz (225g) wholewheat breadcrumbs
16 sage leaves, finely chopped
1 teaspoon allspice berries, crushed
½ teaspoon juniper berries, crushed
½ teaspoon black peppercorns, crushed
¼ teaspoon sea salt

Quarter and thinly slice the onions. Put them in a saucepan with the milk and bay leaves. Cover and simmer for 15 minutes. Remove the bay leaves.

Take the pan from the heat. Mix in the breadcrumbs, sage, spices and seasoning. Cool completely before using to stuff goose, duck or boned pork.

decoction of sage can be used as a mouthwash and breath freshener, and is effective in cases of bleeding gums or excess saliva. Sage is frequently an ingredient of tooth powders; you can also rub sage leaves on teeth and gums to keep them healthy.

An old Welsh manuscript suggests that sage gargle 'should be used in all dangerous seasons when epidemic sore throats prevail; this with God's blessing will preserve you'.

Sage tea has been used to ease rheumatism and other pains in limbs and joints, and has also been recommended for nervous excitement and headaches.

An infusion of sage used as a final rinse when washing the hair will add highlights to dark hair and make grey hair seem darker. It also adds shine and lustre.

 # Salad Burnet

S A N G U I S O R B A   M I N O R

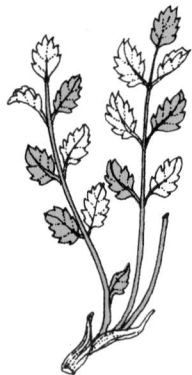

Salad burnet is a native of Britain and Europe and its small red rosettes of flowers can be found growing on chalk hills. Its small, round leaves grow in pairs on slender stems and Turner in the *Newe Herball* of 1551 described them as being 'unto the wings of birdes, standing out as the bird setteth her wings out when she intendeth to fly'. Although little considered in the present day, salad burnet was 'so well known that it needeth no description' in the times of Culpeper, who described it growing wild 'especially in Huntingdon and Northamptonshire, in the meadows there; as also near London by Pancras church, and by a causeway-side in the middle of a field by Paddington'. Early settlers took salad burnet to America where it was grown in gardens and later spread to the wild.

— CULTIVATION —

Salad burnet is a perennial plant which is often the first to appear in early spring and the last to die back in autumn. It also seeds itself like an annual. These self-sown seedlings can be transplanted or left where they are, providing you with an almost year round supply of fresh young leaves.

Salad burnet prefer a chalk or limestone base but will grow in most types of well-drained soil. Keep it weed free and water it during a dry summer. It can be grown from seed sown in spring and the young seedlings should be transplanted to 12 inches (30cm) apart. You can also propagate it by dividing the roots in autumn.

Plants grown specifically for their leaves should have the flower stems taken off as soon as they appear.

— CULINARY USES —

The main culinary use of salad burnet was in summer drinks known as cool tankards, to which it gave a cool, cucumber-like flavour. Use it in wine cups and cocktails, iced fruit drinks and iced lemon tea.

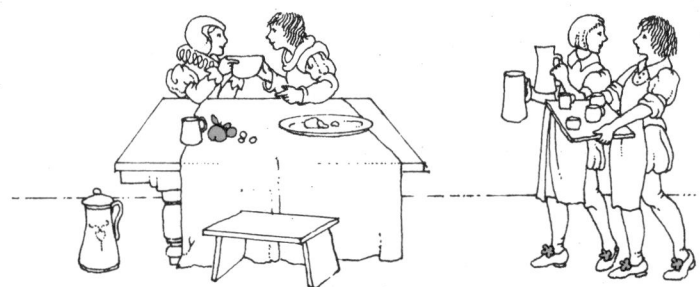

Salad burnet was once grown as a fodder plant on chalky soils for sheep and cattle. It is more nutritive than some grasses, keeps green all winter and survives on poor soil.

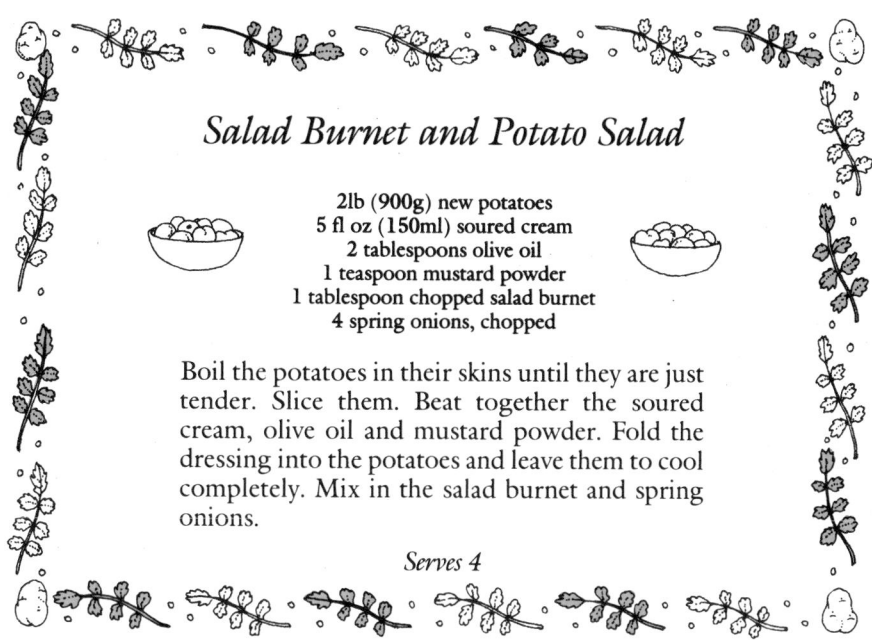

Salad Burnet and Potato Salad

2lb (900g) new potatoes
5 fl oz (150ml) soured cream
2 tablespoons olive oil
1 teaspoon mustard powder
1 tablespoon chopped salad burnet
4 spring onions, chopped

Boil the potatoes in their skins until they are just tender. Slice them. Beat together the soured cream, olive oil and mustard powder. Fold the dressing into the potatoes and leave them to cool completely. Mix in the salad burnet and spring onions.

Serves 4

As its name implies, it is an excellent salad herb if only the youngest leaves from the centre of the plant are used. The outer ones soon become tough and bitter.

A few chopped leaves give a pleasing flavour to cream cheeses. In the absence of sage they can also be used more generously in stuffings for pork and chicken.

— MEDICINAL USES —

The Latin name for salad burnet comes from the word *sanguis* meaning blood, referring to its ability to inhibit bleeding. In Hungary it is called *Chabairje* or 'Chaba's salve' because its juice is said to have cured the wounds of the fifteen thousand sol- diers of King Chaba after a battle fought against his brother. A poultice of the pulped leaves aids the healing of wounds.

A decoction can be used as a lotion for sunburn and eczema. Infused in wine, salad burnet was said to 'quicken the spirits, refresh and clear the heart, and drive away melancholy'. It was also said to prevent infection and cure gout and rheumatism.

— LORE —

In a book claimed to be a translation of one written by King Solomon, it is recorded that magicians were once advised to anoint their swords with the blood of a mole and the juice of burnet leaves.

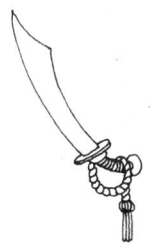

Savory

S A T O R A J A   H O R T E N S I S

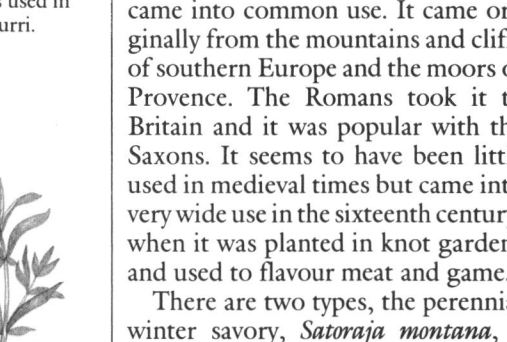

Savory was valued for its hot, spicy flavour before the spices of the East came into common use. It came originally from the mountains and cliffs of southern Europe and the moors of Provence. The Romans took it to Britain and it was popular with the Saxons. It seems to have been little used in medieval times but came into very wide use in the sixteenth century, when it was planted in knot gardens and used to flavour meat and game.

There are two types, the perennial winter savory, *Satoraja montana*, a small woody evergreen shrub; and summer savory, *Satoraja hortensis*, a taller annual, with soft, slender stems and slightly pink-tinged leaves larger than those of winter savory. This variety, according to Gerard, was known as St. Julian's Herb because it grew on St. Julian's Rocks by the Tyrrhenian Sea in Italy.

— CULTIVATION —

Winter savory grows best in a sunny situation and thrives in a poor, rocky soil. It is suitable for growing as a low border around the edge of a garden. Being perennial, winter savory is best propagated by taking cuttings, with a 'heel' attached, in the spring or by root division in autumn. Both the cuttings and the roots can be put directly into their growing positions, about 12 inches (30cm) apart. The plants tend to become shorter and less leafy after two years, so it is best to bring on new ones every other year. Always cut them back after flowering.

Grow summer savory from seed every year, sowing in late spring. It is best to broadcast the seeds thinly over a small patch of fine earth. The plants can be cut back in midsummer for drying, and again in early autumn.

— CULINARY USES —

Savory has always been the 'bean herb' and in small quantities both summer and winter varieties enhance the flavour of green beans and broad beans, as well as dried beans and split peas for soups and casseroles. Small amounts added to cabbage, brussels sprouts and cauliflower not only add flavour but reduce cooking odours.

Hearty beef casseroles benefit from a sprinkling of savory and it can be scattered over roasting joints. In Tudor times it was mixed with breadcrumbs as a coating for meat and fish

GOOSE WITH SAUCE MADAME

'. . . take sage, parsley, hyssop and savory, quinces and pears, garlic and grapes and fill the geese therewith and sew the hole . . .'

The Forme of Cury, fourteenth century

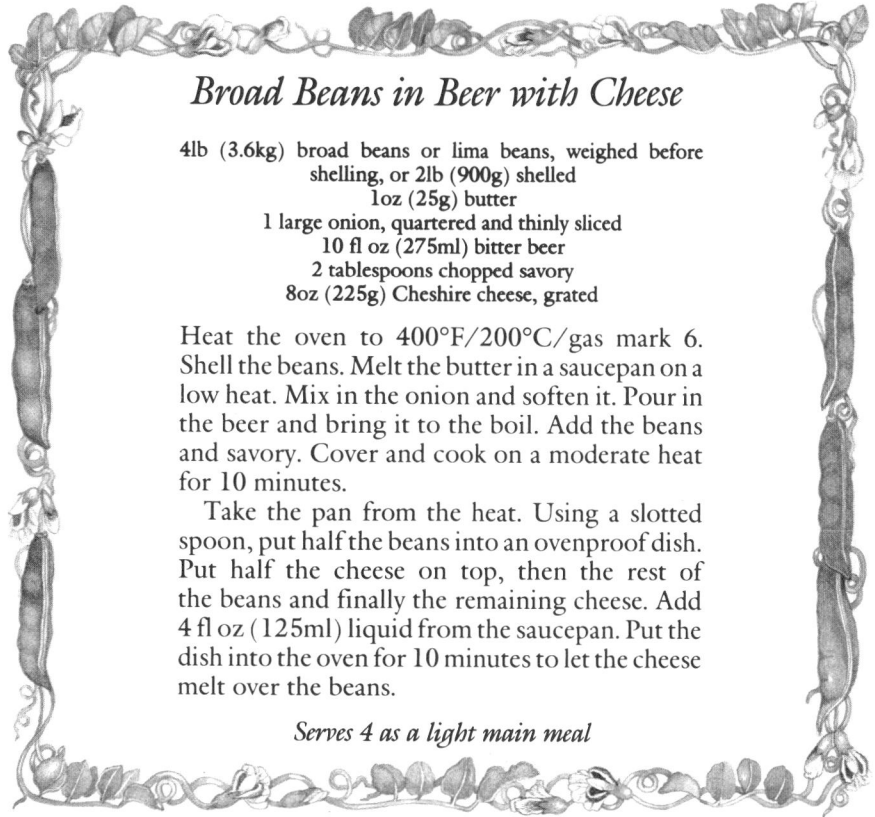

Broad Beans in Beer with Cheese

4lb (3.6kg) broad beans or lima beans, weighed before
shelling, or 2lb (900g) shelled
1oz (25g) butter
1 large onion, quartered and thinly sliced
10 fl oz (275ml) bitter beer
2 tablespoons chopped savory
8oz (225g) Cheshire cheese, grated

Heat the oven to 400°F/200°C/gas mark 6. Shell the beans. Melt the butter in a saucepan on a low heat. Mix in the onion and soften it. Pour in the beer and bring it to the boil. Add the beans and savory. Cover and cook on a moderate heat for 10 minutes.

Take the pan from the heat. Using a slotted spoon, put half the beans into an ovenproof dish. Put half the cheese on top, then the rest of the beans and finally the remaining cheese. Add 4 fl oz (125ml) liquid from the saucepan. Put the dish into the oven for 10 minutes to let the cheese melt over the beans.

Serves 4 as a light main meal

and it is also a fine addition to stuffings, particularly for duck, goose and game.

Used sparingly, savory adds flavour to egg dishes and summer savory is good in green salads.

— MEDICINAL USES —

Both types of savory have the same properties. They have been mainly used as digestive herbs to cure indigestion, flatulence, queasiness of the stomach and spasms.

The pain from bee and wasp stings can be eased by rubbing them with the crushed leaves of savory. A decoction was once used as a bleach for tanned complexions. Culpeper recommended drops made with savory for runny eyes and a poultice made with savory and wheat flour for sciatica.

— LORE —

The Romans considered savory to be an aphrodisiac and both types were supposed to belong to the Satyrs, the goat-like woodland deities of ancient myth.

It is forbidden to use it much in meats. . . . [since it] stirreth him that useth lechery. . . . [but if drunk in wine would] make thee a good meek stomach.

Bankes' Herbal, 1525

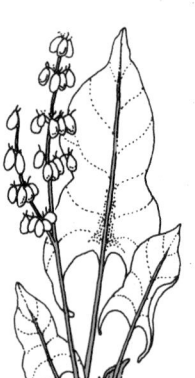

Sorrel has spear-shaped leaves and brown spikes of bloom which, according to one writer, 'need only one ray of sunset to transform these into magnificent flowers'. To many, it may be only an insignificant meadow plant, but to others it is a valued culinary and medicinal herb.

There are two types of sorrel used in the home and kitchen, although there are others that only grow wild. *Rumex acetosa* grows wild throughout Britain, Europe, Asia, Scandinavia and the United States. However, it is given the name of garden sorrel since in Tudor times it was cultivated in herb gardens. In the seventeenth century, the finer-flavoured French sorrel, *Rumex scutatus*, was introduced, and garden sorrel was left to the meadows, although both types are often grown side by side. French sorrel is a native of southern Europe, Germany and Switzerland and has been cultivated in France since very early times.

The Romans cultivated sorrel for culinary use, to balance the effect of rich meats, and they also chewed the leaves to quench thirst, a practice which, according to the English poet John Clare, still carried on in eighteenth-century Northamptonshire. In Tudor times garden sorrel was a pot and salad herb and French sorrel was used in the same ways in the eighteenth century. Interest in sorrel as a culinary herb subsequently declined, but in modern times it has come into its own once more.

— CULTIVATION —

Garden sorrel thrives in a damp soil, but French sorrel prefers a dry soil in an open, sunny situation. Both types are best propagated by dividing the roots in spring or autumn. Plant them with 12 inches (30cm) to spare all round and water them frequently if the weather is dry.

Sorrel can also be grown from seed in spring, in drills 12 inches (30cm) apart. Thin them to 8 inches (20cm) apart when the plants are 2 inches (5cm) high.

To ensure bushy plants with a good supply of leaves, cut off all flower spikes as soon as they appear.

A sorrel plant will last for years, but it is best if the roots are dug and divided every four or five years.

— CULINARY USES —

One of the original uses for sorrel was as a salad herb. Add just a few leaves to fresh summer lettuce, to potato salad and to salads of pulses or pasta. Soups flavoured with sorrel can be light and delicate or thick and nourishing, given substance with such ingredients as lentils, butter beans or potatoes.

Sorrel is a superb complement to eggs. Sauté the chopped leaves in butter before adding them to ome-

SORRILL SAWCE FOR BOYLED CHICKINS

Take verjuice and make it scalding hott, or boyle it if you please then put in a peece of butter and then put in your juice of sorill but after ye juce is in you must not set it over the fire for if you do it will loose couller; so sweeten it, and having sipitts redy cutt lay them rounde the dish, under your chickins, so poure in your sawce; some will put in scalden gooseberrys also; and juce of spinage with the sorill to make it green.

REBECCA PRICE, eighteenth century

lettes, soufflés, roulades and scrambled eggs, or to browned butter and lemon juice as a sauce for poached eggs.

A béchamel sauce flavoured with sorrel purée can also be used for egg dishes and is equally good with boiled or baked ham or gammon, fish, veal or chicken.

Greensauce was once made with sorrel to accompany rich meats and oily fish. Make it today in a similar way to mint sauce, chopping the sorrel very finely and mixing it with vinegar and a little sugar or honey. In Belgium, eels are served with a sorrel sauce.

Add sorrel to stuffings for meat and fish, add a little to give zest to such vegetables as spring greens or broccoli, or beat a few chopped leaves into cream cheese. English author Dorothy Hartley recommended 'dry biscuits stuck together with home-cured bacon and a leaf of sorrel' and a traditional Worcestershire dish was a sweet sorrel pie with a filling of sorrel leaves, brown sugar, raisins and sultanas.

— MEDICINAL USES —

Sorrel is rich in vitamin C and the leaves were often used medicinally by the poor, chewed in spring to prevent scurvy. They were also gathered, for the same reason, by members of an early nineteenth-century Arctic expedition.

It also has antiseptic properties; a hot poultice of sorrel leaves can be used to bring out boils and abcesses and to heal minor wounds.

Sorrel and Haricot Bean Soup

8oz (225g) haricot beans
1 tablespoon sunflower oil
1 bay leaf
1 medium onion, thinly sliced
25 fl oz (725ml) stock
6 oz (75g) sorrel leaves
1 oz (25g) butter
6 fl oz (175ml) soured cream
sea salt and freshly ground black pepper
4 tablespoons chopped parsley

Soak the beans overnight. Boil them in water with the oil, bay leaf and onion. Drain them. Discard the bay leaf. Put the beans and onion through the fine blade of a vegetable mill or rub them through a sieve. Gradually mix in the stock.

Finely chop the sorrel leaves. Melt the butter in a saucepan on a medium heat. Stir in the sorrel leaves and let them soften and 'melt' into the butter. Rub them through a sieve into the beans and stock.

Heat the soup to just below boiling point. Stir in the soured cream. Season to taste. Serve garnished with the parsley.

Serves 4

An infusion of sorrel will ease a sore throat if used as a gargle, and drunk at bedtime helps to allay a fever. As a face wash and also as a drink, it has been known as a treatment for eczema and acne.

According to Parkinson, it was also good for 'quickening up a dull stomacke that is over-loaded with every daies plenty of dishes'.

— HOUSEHOLD USES —

To remove ink stains on a white cloth, rub them with sorrel leaves before washing with soap and water. A decoction of sorrel makes a good cleaner for wicker and bamboo furniture. To clean jars that have contained oil, put in chopped sorrel leaves and a little hot water and shake well.

— LORE —

In early spring, the leaves of garden sorrel are almost tasteless, but later they develop their characteristic acidity due to a high content of binoxalate of potash. This strength of flavour coincides with the arrival of the cuckoo. In country districts it was believed that the cuckoo ate garden sorrel to clear his voice and it was therefore called Cuckoo's Meat or Gowke Meat.

French farmers feed sorrel to cattle as a tonic.

Sweet Cicely

M Y R R H I S   O D O R A T A

Sweet cicely has the sweetest flavour of all the herbs and it is also one of the most beautiful. It grows tall and has large, lacy, slightly furry leaves, pretty umbels of white flowers and stalks sometimes flecked with red. It has a sugared, aniseed-like flavour and a sweet, spicy scent.

Sweet cicely is native to the hills and mountain areas of northern Europe, England, Scotland and Wales, and also to the United States where it was long known and used by the American Indians.

All parts of the plant have been used over centuries to give sweetness in cooking and for aromatic and medicinal properties.

Sweet cicely was confusingly known as sweet chervil by the old herbalists, and its country names include British Myrrh, Sweet Bracken and Shepherd's Needle, referring to the pointed seeds. Its Latin name refers to its myrrh-like scent.

— CULTIVATION —

Sweet cicely is a perennial plant which produces leaves from early spring until late autumn. Older plants can grow up to 5 feet (1.5m) in height,

Sweet cicely is a favourite plant of horses and goats; the American Indians used the crushed roots as a bait to catch wild horses.

Blackcurrant and Redcurrant Tarts

shortcrust pastry made with 8 oz (225g) wholewheat flour
8 oz (225g) blackcurrants
8 oz (225g) redcurrants
4 oz (125g) honey
4 tablespoons chopped sweet cicely
6 fl oz (175ml) thick cream
glacé cherries or angelica, optional

Heat the oven to 400°F/200°C/gas mark 6. Use the pastry to line six foil tartlet tins each 2 inches (5cm) deep and 2 inches (5cm) in diameter. String the currants. Mix them with the honey and sweet cicely. Fill the tartlet cases with the fruits.

Cover each one individually with foil and put them on a baking sheet. Bake the tarts for 25 minutes. Let them cool completely.

Whip the cream. Pipe it on to the tartlets. Decorate with glacé cherries or angelica.

Serves 6

and the more they are cut, the bushier they will become.

It can be propagated by sowing in spring or by dividing the roots in spring or autumn. Sow the seed in medium-rich soil in partial shade, in drills 12 inches (30cm) apart. Seed may take up to nine months to germinate so leave the plants where they are until the second year and then transplant them to 18 inches (45cm) apart. When dividing the roots, discard the long end parts and cut the rest into sections, each with an 'eye'. Plant them 2 inches (5cm) deep and 18 inches (45cm) apart.

— CULINARY USES —

In the sixteenth and seventeenth centuries, sweet cicely was primarily used as a salad herb and it does give a delicious sweet and spicy flavour to green salads, particularly those containing slightly bitter tasting vegetables such as endive or green peppers. It can also be added to cooked cabbage and root vegetables. Herb butter containing sweet cicely is a good accompaniment for poultry and fish.

When sweet cicely was common both wild and in gardens, the roots were dug every autumn to be boiled and served with butter as a vegetable that was thought particularly good for 'aged persons'. American Indians also considered the roots a useful food. Grated raw roots can be added to salads.

Sweet cicely is now most commonly used in sweet dishes, where it not only

The leaves of sweet Chervil are exceeding good, wholesome and pleasant among other sallad herbs.

JOHN GERARD, 1597

... of a sweet, pleasant and spicie hot taste, delightful to many.

JOHN PARKINSON, 1629

gives a delightful flavour but also helps to reduce the acidity of acid fruits. Add it to fruit while it is cooking or to the syrup for a fruit salad. Whip it with cream as a topping or include it in the batter mix for 'sweet pancakes.

The roots were at one time candied as a sweetmeat.

— MEDICINAL USES —

When eaten, sweet cicely acts as a general tonic and appetite stimulant. The seeds are mildly laxative and an infusion of the leaves is a treatment for flatulence. A decoction of the roots was once known as a cure for

consumption, and the candied roots were eaten as protection against plague. The leaves have mild antiseptic properties and were made into an ointment to treat wounds and ulcers.

— HOUSEHOLD USES —

In France the dried leaves were used to stuff pillows and were also laid in the linen cupboard. In England the crushed seeds were rubbed on oak floors and furniture to give gloss and scent.

— LORE —

The distilled water of sweet cicely was once thought to be an aphrodisiac.

Tansy

T A N A C E T U M   V U L G A R E

Tansy is a bitter herb with deeply cut leaves and flowers like small yellow buttons. Its pretty name is a corruption of the Greek word *athenaton*, meaning immortal, given both because its flowers last for so long and because eating the leaves or drinking tansy tea were once thought to promote long life.

Tansy is a native of Europe, Siberia and north-western America and it can now be found growing wild throughout Britain as an escape from monastery gardens. It has been cultivated since Saxon times for its culinary, medicinal and aromatic uses and in Elizabethan times it was much used during Lent and at Easter time.

— CULTIVATION —

Tansy is exceptionally easy to grow; it thrives in almost any soil and, once established, will spread rapidly. It can be propagated from seed or by root division. Sow the seeds in trays in spring. Keep them well watered and plant the seedlings in their growing places in midsummer.

Divide the long, tangled roots in autumn; even the smallest pieces will grow. Set them 2 inches (5cm) deep and 2 feet (60cm) apart. Tansy needs to be confined, like mint, either in its own small bed, in a sunken container or in a space in the herb garden separated from the rest by breeze blocks (cinder blocks) sunk into the soil. If it spreads too far, be ruthless and dig up the unwanted plants in autumn.

The leaves of tansy appear in early spring and are ready for cutting within a month. The plants grow tall during the summer and should be cut back in autumn.

— CULINARY USES —

Tansy is a bitter herb and can be used in stuffings and with rich meats in a similar way to sage. It goes best with pork and poultry. In Ireland it is used to flavour black puddings made with sheep's blood, known as drisheen.

The dish originally known as a Tansy was usually a type of omelette that could be either sweet or savoury and which had a number of forms. It was either coloured with tansy juice or contained the chopped leaves. Very small ones were a garnish for meat or fish; a large Tansy containing bread-crumbs and ground almonds was a complete meal, and there was a sweet version more like a rich custard which was served as a dessert. Other types of Tansy were more pudding-like but also contained the basic egg, ground almond and breadcrumb mixture. Chopped tansy leaves are still used to enhance many egg dishes.

Spiced Roast Pork with Tansy

leg of pork, a piece weighing around 6 lb (2.5kg)
1 teaspoon black peppercorns
1 teaspoon allspice berries
1 teaspoon juniper berries
1 garlic clove
1 tablespoon sea salt
2 tablespoons chopped tansy
2 teaspoons chopped rosemary

Heat the oven to 350°F/180°C/gas mark 4. Score the rind of the pork. Crush together the peppercorns, allspice and juniper berries. Crush the garlic clove with a little of the salt and then mix it with the crushed spices. Add the remaining salt and the tansy and rosemary. Rub the mixture into the pork rind, working it well into the slits. Put the pork on a rack in a roasting tin and roast it in the oven for 2 hours 30 minutes.

— MEDICINAL USES —

Tansy tea was once drunk to cleanse the blood in spring and it is a good general tonic, especially if orange juice and honey are added. It has been recommended for hysteria and other nervous conditions.

A poultice of the leaves will ease bruises and sprains and a fomentation relieves rheumatic pains.

Tansy wine was an old country remedy for stomach troubles, and in

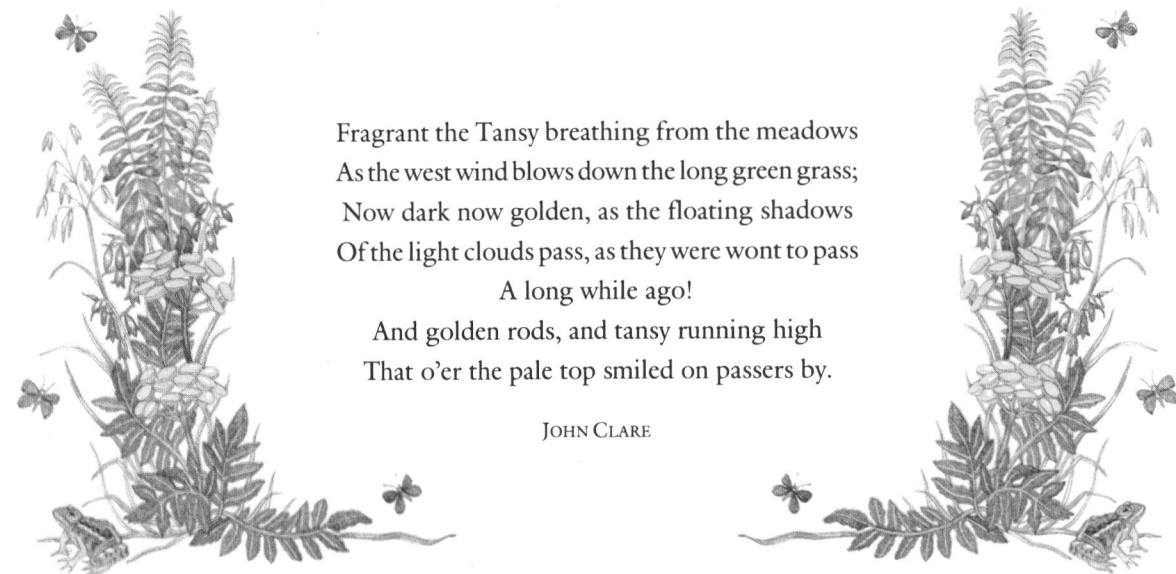

Fragrant the Tansy breathing from the meadows
As the west wind blows down the long green grass;
Now dark now golden, as the floating shadows
Of the light clouds pass, as they were wont to pass
A long while ago!
And golden rods, and tansy running high
That o'er the pale top smiled on passers by.

JOHN CLARE

Soon at Easter commeth
Alleluyah,
With butter, cheese and
tansy.

Old Easter Carol

parts of southern England a sprig was worn in the shoe as a cure for ague.

Buttermilk in which tansy leaves have been steeped soothes the complexion after exposure to the wind and sun.

— SPECIAL USES —

Tansy was a strewing herb, used particularly to keep away flies and lice. It was also hung in kitchens for the same purpose. In courtrooms, churches and other public places it was thought to give protection from the plague.

A green dye for cloth can be made from tansy roots and a yellow or orange dye from the flowers.

The ancient Greeks preserved dead bodies with tansy and it was commonly used in America for the same purpose by the Puritans.

— LORE —

Tansy has long been associated with Lenten and Easter customs. It was at first regarded as a Lenten blood purifier, but came to be associated with the bitter herbs of the Passover. In England, tansy puddings were traditional Easter fare. Archbishops and clergy played handball with the congregation for the prize of a tansy cake. In the north of England, the cakes were offered as forfeits by young men and girls of the village who had stolen each other's shoe buckles. In parts of Italy, however, the giving of tansy was thought to be an insult.

Tansy has been associated with the Virgin Mary. In Roman mythology, it was a herb used by the god Jupiter to bestow immortality.

On Easter Sunday is the
pudding seen,
To Which the Tansy
lends her sober green.

From *The Oxford
Sausage*, a traditional
Easter song.

 # Tarragon

ARTEMESIA DRANUNCULUS

The spiky-leaved tarragon is a strange herb. It has little or no scent but a strong flavour that is warming, spicy and slightly sweet. It is a true herb of summer, loving warm dry weather and going well with cool summer salads.

The origins of tarragon are uncertain. A herbal of 1820 says that it is a native of Siberia and Tartary, and most probably it did come from somewhere in central Asia. It was first introduced to Europe by the Moors who conquered Spain but it remained undiscovered by the rest of Europe until the mid sixteenth century. In the end it was the French who came to love it and use it most of all.

The Moors called tarragon *tharkoum* and the French and English names may be a corruption of this. They could also have come from the Latin *dranunculus* which means 'little dragon'. The plant was so-called because its roots curl back on themselves like a dragon's tail and also because it was used to cure the bites of dogs and 'venomous beasts'.

There are two types of tarragon, French (*Artemesia dranunculus*) and Russian (*Artemesia dranunculoides*). The French has dark green, shiny leaves, it rarely grows taller than 2 feet (60cm) high and its small, round, dull yellow flowers rarely appear. Biting a leaf of French tarragon should make your tongue tingle and this is the variety that the cook should always seek out. Russian tarragon has larger, pale green leaves with no shine. It will grow to a height of 3 feet (1 metre) or more and has small, round, greenish flowers but despite being more vigorous, it lacks the flavour of French tarragon.

— CULTIVATION —

Tarragon enjoys a warm, sunny situation and prefers sandy soil. Gerard wrote that earlier writers 'have reported ... that the seed of flax put into a Raddish root or sea onion, and so set, doth bring forthe this herb Tarragon'.

Tarragon is, in fact, extremely difficult to grow from seed and the best way to propagate it is to divide the roots in spring. You can also take cuttings in spring or summer, putting them into pots of eighty per cent sandy soil and twenty per cent potting medium. For winter use, put a small piece of root into a pot filled with growing medium in the autumn, and keep it on a sunny window sill.

Tarragon roots spread rapidly by means of runners, so the plants grow best if they are divided every autumn. This will produce bushier plants with a good crop of leaves. Cut tarragon right back in the autumn and cover the roots with bracken or straw during the winter to protect them from ground frosts.

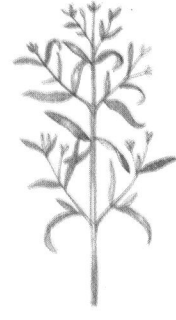

Tarragon was once an ingredient in love potions.

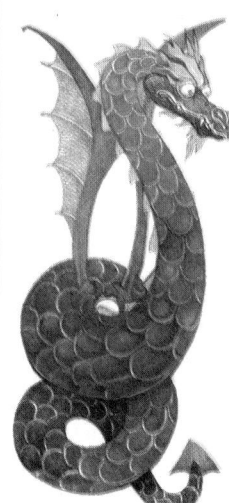

Chicken and Tarragon Salad

3½ lb (1.575kg) roasting chicken
1 sprig tarragon
2 oz (50g) butter
grated rind of a lemon
2 tablespoons chopped tarragon
10 fl oz (575ml) dry cider
2 tablespoons mayonnaise
1 lettuce
1 cucumber

For a garnish:
tarragon sprigs or chopped tarragon

Heat the oven to 350°F/180°C/gas mark 4. Truss the chicken, putting the sprig of tarragon inside. Soften the butter and beat in the lemon rind and chopped tarragon. Spread the butter over the chicken. Put the chicken in a roasting tin and cover it completely with foil. Roast for 1 hour 30 minutes. Remove the foil and pour the cider into the tin. Continue roasting for a further 30 minutes.

Lift out the chicken and let it cool completely. Pour all the juices from the roasting tin into a small bowl and put them into the refrigerator to set. Skim all the fat from the surface. Whisk the set juices with a fork. Whisk in the mayonnaise.

Put a bed of lettuce on a serving dish. Joint or carve the chicken and arrange it on top. Spoon the dressing over the chicken. Arrange cucumber slices round the edge and garnish with tarragon sprigs or chopped tarragon.

Serves 4

— CULINARY USES —

Tarragon is a superb salad herb, highly complimentary to cooling vegetables such as lettuce, corn salad and cucumber. Eggs go well with tarragon. It is one of the *fines herbes* added to omelettes, and eggs baked with cream and tarragon is a well-known first course.

Chicken with tarragon is another classic combination. Lay sprigs on a roasting chicken, add a few chopped leaves to sauté dishes, or use tarragon to flavour aspic for cold chicken. Use it with turkey in the same ways. Lamb can also be flavoured with tarragon: add it to roast and boiled lamb or to a herb butter for lamb chops. Put the same herb butter on grilled fish or sprinkle chopped tarragon leaves into dishes of baked fish.

Tarragon is essential in a perfect Béarnaise sauce and is the distinguishing ingredient in Sauce Tartare.

— MEDICINAL USES —

Although tarragon was once thought to have many medicinal uses, it is now mainly used as a digestive herb which will prevent wind, colic, indigestion and flatulence. The essential oil that it contains, estragole, is appetite-stimulating without being an irritant. It was recommended by Dr Leon Binet, one time Professor of the French Academy of Sciences, as being of great use to 'dyspeptics and patients on a salt-free diet'.

Tarragon root was once used to cure toothache and neuralgia, and the bites of dogs and snakes.

'Tis highly cordial and friend to head, heart and liver.

JOHN EVELYN, 1699

Thyme

THYMUS VULGARIS

The opening summer, the sky,
The shining moorland — to hear
The drowsy bee, as of old,
Hum o'er the thyme.

MATTHEW ARNOLD

Rudyard Kipling described the scent of thyme on the Sussex downs as 'like dawn in Paradise'.

There are many different varieties of thyme and no herb garden should be without at least one. They are all highly fragrant and their tiny leaves and pink or purple heads of flowers make them extremely attractive plants for the front of a herb garden or the edge of a border.

All the thymes are natives of the Mediterranean hills, except one, the wild thyme, which can be found on chalky downs throughout the temperate areas of Europe and Asia and in the mid-western states of America.

The ancient Greeks burnt thyme on the altars of their gods as well as using it medicinally and in the kitchen. The Egyptians and Etruscans employed it in embalming their dead. The Romans used it to flavour cheeses and liqueurs and to scent toilet water. They were responsible for taking it to northern Europe and to Britain, although it was not frequently used there until the Middle Ages.

Common thyme, *Thymus vulgaris*, is the one most used for cooking. Lemon, apple and orange thymes can add their special flavours and wild thyme one that is sweeter. Caraway thyme is also a culinary herb, but most of the other thymes are grown purely for their fragrance and appearance.

— CULTIVATION —

It is said that thyme will only flourish where the air is pure. It grows well in a sandy, well-drained soil that contains some mortar or lime.

Thyme can be propagated by sowing in the spring or by taking cuttings. Sow the seed in drills 8 inches (20cm) apart. When the seedlings are 1 inch (2.5cm) high, put them into small individual pots. Keep them watered, leave them in a sheltered spot, and plant them out the following spring.

Take cuttings in midsummer, each with a 'heel' attached. Set them either

To set down all the particular uses whereunto thyme is applyed were to weary both the writer and the reader . . . we preserve them with all the care we can in our gardens for the sweete and pleasant sents they yield

JOHN PARKINSON, 1629

under a coldframe or in pots under glass, or on a sunny windowsill. Again, plant out the following spring.

Thyme should be planted 10 inches (25cm) apart in an open, sunny situation. Cut the plants back after flowering in summer and again in the autumn. All the thymes are said to flourish near lavender and rosemary, and all are attractive to bees. Wild thyme can be grown as a path, where it will release its scent when trodden.

— CULINARY USES —

A sprig of thyme is an essential part of a *bouquet garni* used to flavour stocks, soups and casseroles. Thyme goes well with lamb, beef and all poultry and game and can be used in casseroles, stews and sauté dishes, stuffings, gravies and sauces. Add sprigs to roasting meats or the chopped leaves to herb butters for serving with grills.

Used sparingly, thyme will enhance egg dishes, particularly baked eggs and omelettes. Many vegetarian dishes, particularly those made with nuts or pulses, also benefit from a sprinkling of thyme added at the beginning of cooking. It can be cooked with vegetables, particularly green beans and root vegetables. In Spain and Italy, sprigs of thyme are added to pickled olives and gherkins and to jars of olives preserved in oil.

Lemon thyme is excellent with fish, lamb and poultry. With orange thyme, it can be added to salads and to fruit dishes.

Caraway thyme, *Thymus herba-barona*, was the traditional herb for a baron of beef, used not only to flavour but to prevent the meat from going off and to mask bad flavours if it had.

— MEDICINAL USES —

Both common thyme and wild thyme can be used medicinally and have similar properties.

An infusion of thyme has long been regarded as a general tonic 'to conduce the health of man's body'. Drunk cold in summer it is reviving and soothing. Hot, it is a good digestive that will ease colic, indigestion and flatulence. A hot infusion sweetened with honey is recommended for all coughs and chest colds, and a stronger decoction

Wild thyme is a tonic to sheep and goats, flavouring the meat as well as the milk.

French Beans with Thyme and Cashew Nuts

1 lb (450g) French beans
3 tablespoons sunflower oil
3 oz (75g) cashew nuts
1 garlic clove, finely chopped
1 tablespoon chopped thyme

Top and tail the beans. Boil them in lightly salted water for 12 minutes, or until they are just tender. Drain them.

Heat the oil in a frying pan on a medium heat. Put in the cashew nuts and stir until they are golden brown. Remove them. Raise the heat. Put in the beans and garlic and stir until the garlic begins to brown. Mix in the nuts and thyme and take the pan from the heat.

Serves 4

for whooping cough. The infusion can also be used as a gargle for sore throats. A few drops of oil of thyme in boiling water make a good inhalant for a stuffy nose. The powdered leaves taken as snuff will also clear the head.

A decoction of thyme added to the bath stimulates the circulation and skin. Rubbed into the scalp it helps to stimulate hair growth and prevent dandruff.

Thyme tea is said to be good for a hangover and the Romans used it as a remedy for melancholy. In the seventeenth century, thyme soup was thought to be a cure for shyness.

— HOUSEHOLD USES —

The Greeks and Romans fumigated rooms and public places by burning thyme, a practice which also drove away fleas and insects. In sixteenth-century England, sprigs of thyme were laid amongst furs and other winter clothes to keep away fleas and moths.

The scented varieties of thyme can all be used in pot-pourris and sweet-bags.

— LORE —

To the Greeks and, later, in medieval times, thyme was a symbol of courage. Lancastrian ladies, at the time of the English Wars of the Roses, embroidered a bee hovering over thyme on the corners of scarves which were given to their knights to wear in battle or at tournaments. Before this sprigs of thyme were given to knights going on Crusades.

The Greeks also used thyme as a

symbol of elegance and to say that anyone 'smelt of thyme' was a way of expressing praise for his style.

An old Greek legend claimed that thyme sprang from the tears of Helen of Troy. Others said that it was one of the fragrant herbs that made up the bed of the Virgin Mary.

In Wales, thyme was placed on graves. In other places, girls would wear sprigs of thyme, mint and lavender to bring them sweethearts.

Wild thyme was said to be a favourite plant of the fairies. In Scotland it is known as the Badge of the Drummond clan. In the south of France, before the French revolution, thyme was a symbol of extreme republicanism; receiving a sprig of wild thyme was an invitation to a republican meeting.

Woodruff

G A L I U M   O D O R A T A

Hanged up in houses in the heate of sommer doth very well attemper the aire, coole and make fresh the place, to the delight and comfort of such as are therein.

JOHN GERARD 1597

Sweet woodruff is a small, delicate herb which smells like vanilla when fresh and new-mown hay when dried. It has tiny white flowers and bright green leaves growing in ruffs up short, thin stems which account for half its name. The other half comes from the fact that it grows on the edges of woods.

In Germany, it is called 'master of the woods', or *Maitrank* because it is added to a maytime drink.

Woodruff grows wild all over Britain, Europe, Scandinavia, in parts of Asia and the United States, apart from the extreme south. Since the Middle Ages it has been used both medicinally and in the kitchen.

— CULTIVATION —

Woodruff grows best in places that are similar to its wild habitat, under trees if possible, and in partial shade. It can be grown from seed but it may take a very long time to germinate. Sow it in trays under glass and plant out the seedlings when they are about 1½ inches (4cm) high. Woodruff likes a rich but not heavy soil, preferably dressed with leaf mould. It can also be propagated by pulling off pieces of the roots in spring. Set them 4 inches (10cm) apart and water them well. Once established, woodruff will spread by self-sowing and also by its roots. A covering of leaf mould, bracken or straw helps woodruff to survive cold weather.

— CULINARY USES —

Woodruff has mainly been used to flavour drinks, for the taste and 'to make a man merrie'. In Germany it is put into the Maibowle, a Rhine wine

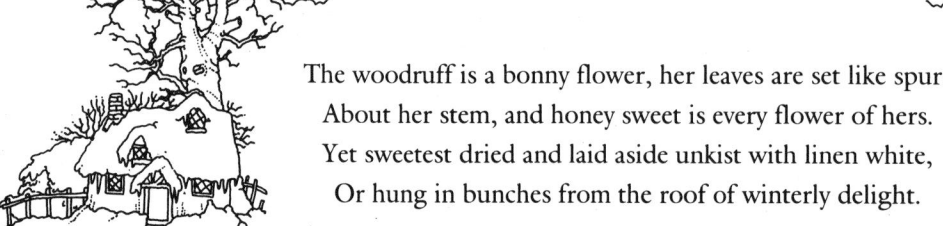

The woodruff is a bonny flower, her leaves are set like spurs
About her stem, and honey sweet is every flower of hers.
Yet sweetest dried and laid aside unkist with linen white,
Or hung in bunches from the roof of winterly delight.

ANON

cup, on May Day. The French steep it in champagne and the Swiss in Benedictine, cognac, hock and vodka. Sprigs can be added to all types of wine cups and fruit cups or to plain apple juice to give a vanilla-like flavour. Woodruff tea is calming and soothing and you can also give a special flavour to China tea by adding a sprig of woodruff to the pot.

Wherever a vanilla pod is called for in a recipe, a woodruff sprig can be substituted. Use it to flavour custards, sweet sauces, ice-creams and zabaglione.

— MEDICINAL USES —

Woodruff tea is mainly used to help insomnia and to calm the nerves. It will ease nervous headaches, migraine and menstrual pains. It is also thought to help all functions of the liver and to relieve fevers. The distilled water was once applied to soothe the complexion after exposure to the wind and sun.

The bruised leaves will bring out bruises on the skin and in medieval and Tudor times they were laid over wounds and cuts as a salve.

— SPECIAL USES —

Dried woodruff, with its scent of new-mown hay, was once used in great quantities for stuffing into pillows and mattresses, for hanging in rooms and for freshening clothes and linen. Leaves were placed between the pages of books and in Georgian England, a whorl of leaves would be placed in the back of a pocket watch so the fragrance could be inhaled when the wearer was in a stuffy or unpleasant atmosphere.

Dried woodruff is an ingredient of snuffs and the plant is used in perfumery as a fixative.

— LORE —

Woodruff was part of traditional decoration of churches at festivals, particularly on the days of St Barnabas and St Peter, when it was hung up with lavender and roses.

It is reported to be put into wine, to make a man merry, and to be good for the heart and liver, it prevaileth in wounds.

JOHN GERARD, 1597

It is good for healing all sickness that comes from heat.

Hortus sanitatis

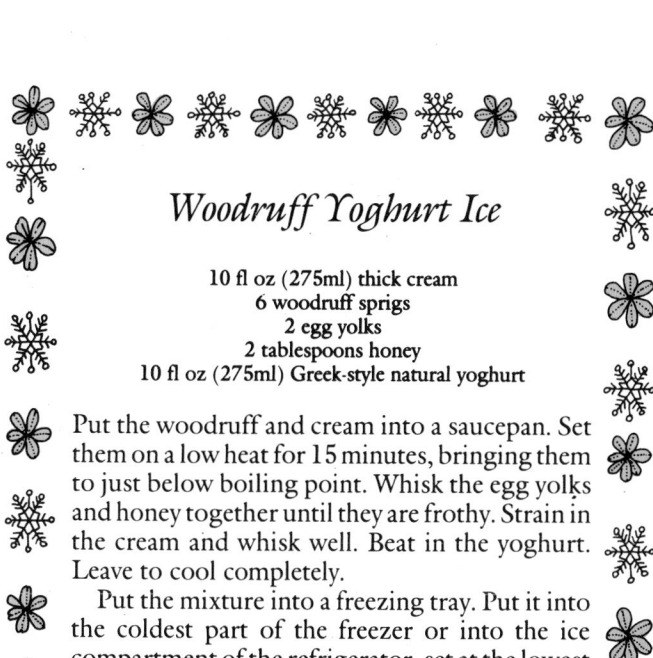

Woodruff Yoghurt Ice

10 fl oz (275ml) thick cream
6 woodruff sprigs
2 egg yolks
2 tablespoons honey
10 fl oz (275ml) Greek-style natural yoghurt

Put the woodruff and cream into a saucepan. Set them on a low heat for 15 minutes, bringing them to just below boiling point. Whisk the egg yolks and honey together until they are frothy. Strain in the cream and whisk well. Beat in the yoghurt. Leave to cool completely.

Put the mixture into a freezing tray. Put it into the coldest part of the freezer or into the ice compartment of the refrigerator, set at the lowest temperature. Freeze to a slush, which takes 2–3 hours. Beat well to break up the ice particles. Put the ice-cream into a plastic container, cover and freeze completely, about 4 hours. Before serving, put the ice-cream into the refrigerator for 45 minutes.

Serves 6

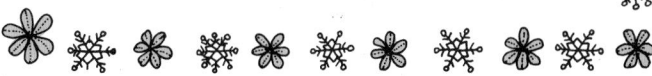

Spices

Allspice

PIMENTO OFFICINALIS

Allspice berries have a delicate scent and a flavour that is a tantalizing and indefinable mixture of other spices. It enhances food rather than overpowers and is one of the most versatile of spices to have in the kitchen. Yet since its first discovery, which was almost by accident, it has been somewhat neglected. No battles have been fought for it and no companies set up to market it.

Allspice is a native of Jamaica and other Caribbean islands, and of the tropical parts of Central America. In his search for pepper and other spices, Christopher Columbus twice passed through the Caribbean and noticed the trees with their sweetly scented evergreen leaves, but as the fruits were not ripe he did not realize their potential value. Forty years later, the Spaniards, looking for pepper that they heard grew in Jamaica, discovered allspice and named it *pimienta de Jamaica*, or Jamaican pepper. It soon became identified as pimento, somewhat confusingly, as pimientos was the name already given to chillies by the Spaniards.

No allspice reached England until 1601, when it was looked on as a pharmaceutical curiosity, but after Jamaica was taken over by the English in 1655, regular shipments to London gradually increased. By the nineteenth century it was a popular spice in everyday domestic cookery, but still not regarded as exotic. However, allspice was much used by early American settlers as it was found growing wild in their own country.

— CULTIVATION —

Most of the world's allspice still comes from Jamaica. Attempts to transplant it to Australia, Ceylon, India and Singapore have resulted in flourishing trees but no berries.

In Jamaica, allspice is grown in plantations on hills overlooking the sea. The trees begin to fruit when they are seven years old and may continue to be productive for a hundred years.

The berries are picked while they are still green since they lose their aroma as they ripen. Men and boys climb the trees, break off the brittle branches and throw them down to the women and children who strip off the berries. The berries are first packed into sacks and left to 'sweat' for a few days. After this they are spread out on concrete platforms to dry in the sun. They are turned frequently and swept into huts at night and when it rains. When dry, they are cleaned in a rotating barrel before packing.

— CULINARY USES —

Allspice is available ground and whole. Since the flavour deteriorates quickly when it is ground it is best to buy whole berries and either crush them with a pestle and mortar or keep them in a pepper mill for immediate use when ground spice is called for.

All types of pickled and preserved meats benefit from the flavour of allspice. Add the crushed berries to brines and dry salting mixtures for pork, beef, lamb and duck. The Arawaks, the original natives of Jamaica, used allspice for this purpose. The cured meats were known as *boucan*, and the European pirates who ate them in such quantities on board ship became known as *boucaniers*.

Pickled or salt fish, dill pickles, sauces and ketchups are all improved by a hint of allspice, and it is frequently added to commercially made sausages, pork pies and hamburgers. In Jamaica

Roast Duck with Apple Stuffing

4 lb (1.8kg) duck
2 large Bramley apples
1 small onion, finely chopped
15 fl oz (425ml) stock, made from the duck giblets
3 oz (75g) fresh wholewheat breadcrumbs
8 allspice berries, crushed
8 black peppercorns, crushed
4 sage leaves, chopped
4 tablespoons brandy
2 teaspoons fine sea salt
2 tablespoons wholewheat flour

Heat the oven to 350°F/180°C/gas mark 4. Peel, core and finely chop the apples. Put the onion into a saucepan with 5 fl oz (150ml) stock. Bring it to the boil, cover and simmer for 10 minutes, until the onion is soft and the stock is reduced by half. Take the pan from the heat and mix in the onions, apples, breadcrumbs, allspice and pepper, sage and 2 tablespoons brandy.

Put the resulting stuffing into the duck. Truss the duck, prick the skin all over with a fork and rub it all over with the sea salt. Put the duck on a rack in a roasting tin and cover it with foil. Roast the duck for 1 hour 30 minutes. Remove the foil. Dredge the duck with flour and baste it. Return it, uncovered, to the oven for 30 minutes. Transfer the duck to a carving plate.

Pour away the fat and set the roasting tin on top of the stove on a moderate heat. Pour in the remaining stock and bring it to the boil, stirring in any residue from the bottom of the tin. Simmer while the duck is carved and arranged on a serving plate with the stuffing. Serve the gravy separately.

Serves 4

it is an ingredient of soups, stews and curries and is a frequent seasoning for sweet potatoes.

Early American settlers added allspice to cakes, cookies and pumpkin pies for its sweet, mild flavour. Fruit salads can be given a grinding of the fresh berries. Sprinkle allspice over coffee or infuse the whole berries in hot punches and toddies.

— MEDICINAL USES —

Allspice is used as a flavouring agent in many tonics and medicines. Oil from the leaves dropped on to a sugar cube will relieve flatulence and other stomach upsets. It can also be used as a rub for rheumatic pains and sprains.

— SPECIAL USES —

Allspice oil is used in the making of perfume and soap and other toilet preparations which bear the label 'spice'. The crushed berries can be added to pot-pourris and sweet bags.

From 1880 until 1930, wood from allspice trees was commonly used to make walking sticks.

During the Napoleonic Wars, Russian soldiers put allspice berries in their boots to keep their feet warm.

— LORE —

In Jamaica it is said that allspice trees will only reproduce themselves on that island, but this belief is not true.

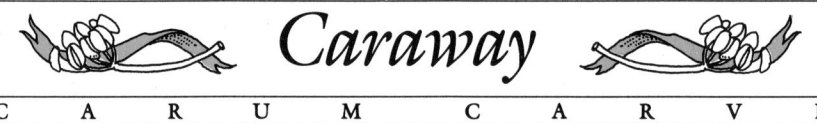

Caraway

C   A   R   U   M   C   A   R   V   I

Caraway, with its thin, brown, sweetly spiced seeds is not an exotic spice. It comes from an umbelliferous herb that can be grown in gardens in temperate areas and is a native of Britain, Canada and the United States, northern and central parts of Europe and Asia, Siberia, the Middle East and Scandinavia. It was once cultivated on a large scale in the east of England and most of the world's supplies now come from Holland.

Caraway was well known to the Greeks and Romans. It was used by the ancient Egyptians and also in Babylon in the eighth century. Karawya was a name given to it by the ancient Arabs.

Medieval Europe did not appreciate caraway as much as the expensive imported spices, but it was used frequently in the eighteenth century when application of the other spices was far less extravagant.

— CULTIVATION —

Caraway can be grown in herb gardens from seed sown in late summer. Sow in warm, light, well-drained soil in drills 15 inches (37cm) apart and thin the plants in spring to 18 inches (45cm) apart. The seeds will ripen the following autumn. Scatter some on the ground when harvesting and they will provide new plants and seed the following year.

Oil of caraway is used in the making of perfumes and soaps. The crushed seeds can be added to pot-pourri.

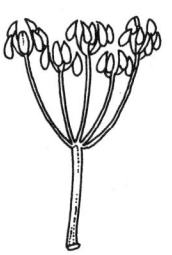

One of the most frequent uses of caraway has been in bread, cakes and biscuits. In Norway and Sweden and other European countries the seeds are put into black bread and rye bread, and caraway bread has been well-liked in Jewish communities. Caraway buns, sometimes known as wigs, and biscuits were once a favourite English Lenten food and small shell-shaped cakes were offered with wine to afternoon guests. In country districts, rich caraway cakes raised with yeast were popular at harvest and sheepshearing suppers.

In Scotland a bowl of caraway seeds was put on the table as a dip for bread and butter. For some reason, now forgotten, they were known as 'salt water jelly'. Following this tradition, caraway seeds can be put into sandwiches.

When sugar-coated, the seeds become caraway comfits. These were sprinkled over roasted apples as a dessert in medieval times. Add a few seeds to an apple pie and the flavour will be similar.

Caraway seeds can also be added sparingly to savoury soups and casseroles. They go well with root vegetables, including beetroot, add good flavour to sauerkraut. When put in a pan with boiling cabbage, they both improve the flavour and reduce kitchen odours.

Country wine or brandy can be flavoured with caraway seeds. Oil of caraway is used commercially to flavour the liqueur known as kummel.

Carraway confects, once only dipped in sugar, and a spoonful of them eaten in the morning fasting, and as many after each meal, is a most admirable remedy for those that are troubled with wind.

NICHOLAS CULPEPER, 1649

The seed is much used to be put among baked fruit, or into bread cakes, etc., to give them a rellish. It is also made into comfites and taken for cold or wind in the body, which are served to the table with fruit.

JOHN PARKINSON, 1629

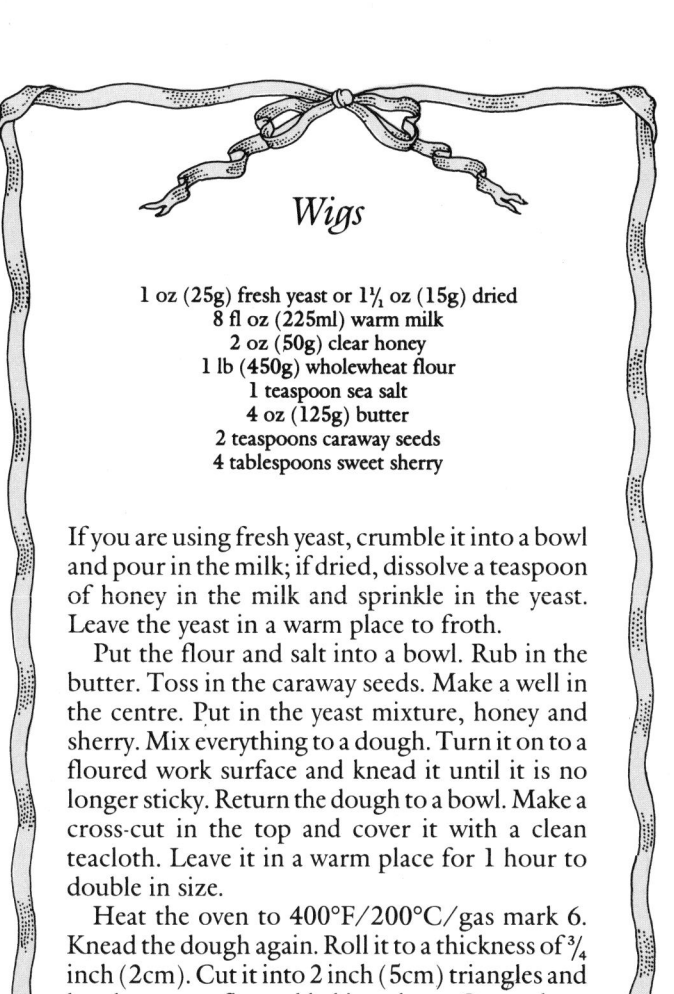

Wigs

1 oz (25g) fresh yeast or 1¹⁄₁ oz (15g) dried
8 fl oz (225ml) warm milk
2 oz (50g) clear honey
1 lb (450g) wholewheat flour
1 teaspoon sea salt
4 oz (125g) butter
2 teaspoons caraway seeds
4 tablespoons sweet sherry

If you are using fresh yeast, crumble it into a bowl and pour in the milk; if dried, dissolve a teaspoon of honey in the milk and sprinkle in the yeast. Leave the yeast in a warm place to froth.

Put the flour and salt into a bowl. Rub in the butter. Toss in the caraway seeds. Make a well in the centre. Put in the yeast mixture, honey and sherry. Mix everything to a dough. Turn it on to a floured work surface and knead it until it is no longer sticky. Return the dough to a bowl. Make a cross-cut in the top and cover it with a clean teacloth. Leave it in a warm place for 1 hour to double in size.

Heat the oven to 400°F/200°C/gas mark 6. Knead the dough again. Roll it to a thickness of ¾ inch (2cm). Cut it into 2 inch (5cm) triangles and lay them on a floured baking sheet. Cover them with the cloth again and leave them in a warm place for 20 minutes. Bake the buns for 20 minutes or until they are risen and golden brown. Cool them on a wire rack.

Makes about 20

— MEDICINAL USES —

A mild infusion of caraway seeds was once used in the same way as dill, to calm fractious children. It is a pleasant aid to digestion that can be drunk after meals to tone the whole of the digestive tract. It was for this reason that the seeds were originally put into bread and cakes.

Poultices of the seeds have been used to lessen the pain of sprains, to bring out bruises and to hold against the ear for earache. Caraway comfits were once thought to be good for the eyesight and Pliny recommended eating the seeds to brighten a pale complexion. Caraway is now used commercially to flavour otherwise unpleasant medicines.

— LORE —

It was once thought that caraway would prevent the theft of any object that contained it. More romantically, it was an ingredient in love potions believed to prevent infidelity in lovers. The master of a farm would give caraway cake to his workers as a way of binding their loyalty. It was also fed to pigeons and chickens to prevent them from straying.

Cardamom

ELETTARIA CARDAMOMUM

Smell a jar of cardamom and you are reminded of sweet, refreshing sherbet drinks. It has an effervescent smell and a spicy flavour which blends with both sweet and savoury ingredients.

Cardamom is native to India and south-east Asia; it is a member of the ginger family and one of the world's most important spices. In India it is called the Queen of Spices, pepper being the King.

In ancient Greece and Rome, cardamom was an important ingredient in medicines and perfumes. During the Dark Ages, it was taken through Constantinople to be traded for salt and meat in Venice. It was the favourite spice of the Vikings who used it in their festival cakes and wrote about it in their great sagas known as the Eddas. Cardamom reached Europe in the early thirteenth century. In England it was essentially a summer spice, used to flavour dishes that were coloured green with herbs.

— CULTIVATION —

Cardamom thrives in moist, tropical areas. India is the world's largest exporter, but cardamom is also grown commercially in Vietnam, Thailand, Sri Lanka, Tanzania and parts of South America.

Cardamom bears yellowish flowers that grow on horizontally spreading stems. The fruits, which ripen throughout the year, are harvested by cutting them off the branches with sharp scissors when they are three-quarters ripe. They are kiln-dried on

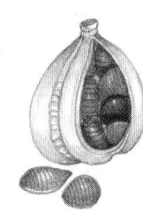

Cardamom is sold in its pods to preserve the flavour of the small black seeds. The pods are either green or straw-coloured and the paler they are, the better the quality.

trays in the drying house. Hot air is blown at them and they are occasionally turned. The process is deliberately slow in order to preserve the essential oils. When the pods are still hot, they are rubbed over wire or bamboo trays to remove the stalks and flowers. The larger, rounded pale green pods always fetch the highest price.

— CULINARY USES —

In India and Sri Lanka, cardamom is an important ingredient in curry powders and the spice mixture garam masala. Very often, the seeds are roasted before they are ground to bring out their flavour. Add them to dishes of lentils and pulses, to rice, chicken and meat.

The Scandinavians still use ground cardamom in cakes and in Danish pastries. Use it also to add distinctive flavour to pancakes, waffles and spice biscuits. Sugar which has been kept in a closed container with crushed cardamom pods is ideal for sprinkling over pastries and other desserts and the pods can be simmered in the syrup for poached fruit or fruit salad.

In many Arab countries coffee is flavoured with cardamom and it can also be added to chocolate drinks. The essential oil is used commercially in bitters and liqueurs.

— MEDICINAL USES —

An infusion of crushed cardamom seeds drunk after meals acts as a digestive. In India the seeds are chewed with betel nut for the same reason. The infusion will also check nausea and morning sickness and sweeten the breath. Used as a gargle, it eases sore throat, hoarseness and pharyngitis and protects from influenza.

Eating cardamom crushed with honey every day was once thought to improve the eyesight; however, it was also said that eating too much cardamom would cause impotence.

— LORE —

In the east, cardamom was an ingredient in love potions. An old Persian recipe for regaining the affections of a roving husband instructed that cardamom, cloves and cinnamon be placed in a jar while a chapter of the Koran was read backwards several times. The jar was filled with rosewater and the husband's shirt was steeped in it, together with a parchment on which was written his name and those of four angels. They were all heated over the fire and as they boiled, the husband was said to return.

In France and America cardamom is used in perfumery. It was a constituent of face masks worn overnight by Roman women and was also an ingredient in the original type of pomander.

Spiced Coffee and Chocolate Drink

8 fl oz (225ml) milk
2 cardamom pods, bruised
1 teaspoon instant coffee
½ oz (15g) chocolate flake or grated chocolate

Put the milk and cardamom pods into a saucepan. Set them on a low heat and bring them gradually to just below boiling point. Put the coffee into a mug. Strain on the milk and stir. Crumble in the flake and do not stir any more.

Serves 1

 # Cayenne Pepper

C A P S I C U M   F R U T E S C E N S

The light orange powder that we call cayenne pepper is one of the hottest of all spices, with a bitter scent and sharp, clean taste. It is produced by grinding the dried fruits of one of the many varieties of *Capsicum*, which include sweet red and green peppers.

Capsicum frutescens and the smaller variety *Capsicum frutescens minimum* are native to tropical America, but have been grown in the West Indies, India, Japan, south-east Asia and some parts of Africa. They were grown during Inca times in South America and it is said that Christopher Columbus first found them in Cuba. It is possible that they were introduced to Europe by him, but another story is that they were brought first to England from India in 1548.

In English eighteenth-century recipe books cayenne is called 'chyan' or red pepper and at the time it was just as popular as black pepper.

The name comes from the port of Cayenne in French Guiana where the spice was once grown.

— CULTIVATION —

Capsicum frutescens grows to about 3 inches (7.5cm) long and *Capsicum frutescens minimum* to about ¾ inch (2cm). Both are initially green and ripen to a deep orange-red. They are picked when ripe and dried and the pods and seeds are then ground together to make a light orange-red powder with a fairly coarse texture. African cayenne pepper may be lighter and more yellow in colour.

— CULINARY USES —

The clean, sharp flavour of cayenne pepper makes it ideal for adding

Trout Marinated in Lime Juice

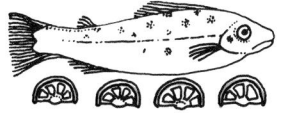

4 trout
grated rind and juice of a lime
4 tablespoons olive oil
¼ teaspoon cayenne pepper
3 tablespoons chopped parsley
3 tablespoons chopped mint

Clean the trout and cut their tails into V-shapes. Cut three diagonal slits in the side of each trout, running backwards and downwards from head to tail. Beat together the rind and juice of the lime, the olive oil and cayenne pepper. Lay the trout on a large, flat dish and brush them inside and out with the marinade, working it into the slits. Fill the slits with the herbs. Leave the trout for at least 2 hours at room temperature.

Heat the grill to high and if you have an open wire grill-rack, cover it with foil. Lay the trout on the hot rack and grill them for about 5 minutes on each side, so they are browned and cooked through.

Serves 4

hotness but not taste to dishes of a delicate flavour. It is used in many parts of the world in both hot and cold dishes of fish and seafood and is ideal for salad dressings.

In India and the Middle East, cayenne pepper is added to hot, spicy dishes of both meats and pulses. It also features in the Creole cooking of the United States.

In western cooking it is added to classic brown sauces, béchamel and Hollandaise sauces and to creamy soups. It is the ideal seasoning for delicately flavoured vegetables such as cauliflower and asparagus, and also for egg and cheese dishes.

Cayenne pepper can be very hot, so use only a small pinch at first and add it at the beginning of cooking so it loses its 'raw' flavour. Store it in light-tight containers, as light can destroy its flavour.

— MEDICINAL USES —

A pinch of cayenne pepper added to an infusion of yarrow, peppermint and elderflowers is a good remedy for colds and influenza. In the West Indies it is added to a mixture of cucumber, onions, lime juice and Madeira, used as a cure for weak digestion and loss of appetite.

Cayenne has been used in treating alcohol addiction and it is also an ingredient of various tonics.

Chillies

C A P S I C U M F R U T E S C E N S

Burn dried chillies slowly in a frying pan to fumigate a room.

Chillies are small capsicums which are used more as a flavouring or garnish for dishes and sauces than as a vegetable. They can be green, red or yellow and vary in flavour from hot and pungent to sweet and mild. All colours are sold fresh both in their countries of origin and in the countries which import them: red chillies are also sold dried. Chilli powder is made from dried ground chillies mixed with ground cumin, oregano and garlic to make a spice less hot than cayenne pepper and with more flavour.

Chillies are native to Mexico where they were grown nine thousand years ago. Chilli is the original Mexican name and although the Conquistadores changed it to *chili* it was still pronounced the same. From Mexico, chillies were taken into what is now Texas and down into South America. Further north, they were used by the American Indians. The Arawaks and the Caribs who migrated to the West Indies from what is now Venezuela took chillies with them and Christopher Columbus found them growing in Hispaniola in 1492.

Chillies were planted in Spain in the sixteenth century and soon afterwards in Portugal. From here they were taken to India where they rapidly became among the most important spices. They were soon bought by the Arabs who transported them along the old spice routes and adopted them for their own cuisine. The Portuguese took chillies to Japan and they have also been popular in the Szechuan region of China, where it is claimed they are indigenous.

— CULTIVATION —

Chillies are now grown by three-quarters of all the spice-producing countries. They flourish in warm, humid climates where they are grown mostly as annuals. They are picked when ripe and sold either fresh or dried. Some varieties are ground to make chilli powder or cayenne pepper.

— CULINARY USES —

Whole fresh chillies should be cut with care. Remove the cores with a small, pointed knife, slice the chillies in half lengthways and scrape out and discard all the seeds. Do not let the juice squirt in your eyes and do not rub your eyes or lick your fingers after handling chillies.

Fresh chillies can be added to eastern-style curries and to many Latin-American and Mexican dishes. They are chopped for use in stew-type dishes and hearty soups and in sauces for fish and shellfish. Sliced into rounds or chopped, they are a garnish for Mexican tortillas, fried or poached eggs and omelettes.

Whole dried chillies are often used in western countries to flavour pickl-

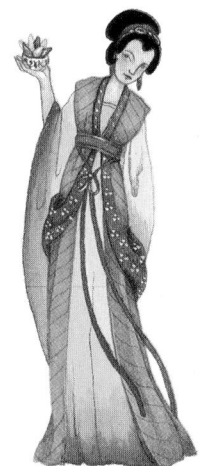

Pickled Peach Slices

4 lb peaches
15 fl oz (425ml) white wine vinegar
6 dried red chillies
1 teaspoon cloves
1 teaspoon allspice berries
4 inch (10cm) cinnamon stick,
1½ lb (675g) demerara or coarse sugar

Scald, stone and slice the peaches. Put the vinegar into the pan with the remaining ingredients. Stir on a low heat to dissolve the sugar. Bring the vinegar to the boil. Cover and simmer for 15 minutes. Put in the peaches and simmer, uncovered, for 2 minutes. Lift out the peaches with a perforated spoon and put them into warm preserving jars. Boil the vinegar for 10 minutes to thicken it. Remove the cinnamon stick. Pour the vinegar over the peach slices, allowing an equal amount of spices into each jar. Cover immediately. Leave for three weeks before opening.

Fills three 1 lb (450g) jars

ing syrups and vinegars and also salad oils. Soaked and crushed, they can be a substitute for fresh chillies in cooked dishes. Crumbled red chillies feature in Japanese cookery. In the Szechuan province of China, chilli sauce is more often used than whole chillies.

Chilli powder was invented in the 1860s. One story says that it was the idea of an emigrant Englishman trying to create a substitute for curry powder. It was frequently used in America by chuck-wagon cooks on cattle drives, who are said to have invented chilli con carne partly for reasons of keeping the food fresh, as they had noticed that the American Indians used chillies to preserve meat.

Tabasco sauce was first made in Louisiana near the Mississippi Delta by a banker called Edward McIlhenny, who had been made bankrupt by the Civil War. It is made with ripe red pepper, ground and soaked in spirit vinegar and left to ferment in oak casks for three years.

— MEDICINAL USES —

Fresh chillies are rich in vitamin C. In India they are used as an appetite stimulant. An infusion of dried or ground chillies is a treatment for chills and fever. Added to ointments they make a rub for aching muscles.

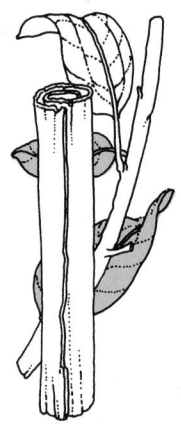

Cinnamon

CINNAMOMUM ZEYLANICUM

Cinnamon, with its softly sweet scent and flavour, has been valued since ancient times. It is native to south-east Asia, India and China and is now grown mainly in Sri Lanka, India, Indonesia and South Vietnam.

Cinnamon is a member of the laurel family with shiny, dark evergreen leaves, white flowers and round berries resembling olives. It is not the fruits that are harvested for use as a spice, but the fragrant bark. Its name comes from the Malay *kayu manis* meaning sweet wood. There are actually two types. *Cinnamomum zeylanicum*, or Ceylon cinnamon, is sold in the characteristic rolled sticks and is also ground to make a pale brown, mildly aromatic powder. This is popular in many parts of the world including Mexico and the United Kingdom. *Cinnamomum cassia*, known commonly as cassia or, in Britain, cinnamon bark, has a stronger, more bitter flavour and is sold either ground as a red-brown powder or as pieces of bark. It is the more popular variety in the United States where it is known as cinnamon. Ground cinnamon may have a certain amount of cassia mixed with it and this is the type preferred by the food-processing industry. The French word *canelle* covers both cinnamon and cassia and throughout history the terms have been interchangeable.

The ancient Egyptians used cinnamon in cosmetics and for embalming. The Pharoahs sent out ships to what they thought were the cinnamon-growing lands of Ethiopia and Somalia. The spice never grew there, in fact, but was taken there on rafts by the Indonesians. The Queen of Sheba gave cinnamon to King Solomon and it was one of the spices used to make holy ointment for the Tabernacle. The Phoenicians and the Romans took cinnamon to Greece and the Romans bought their supplies from what is now Sri Lanka.

In 1536 the Portuguese captured Sri Lanka and demanded a payment of cinnamon from the king. They dominated trade until the Dutch took the island from them in 1636. They began cultivating cinnamon there on a large scale, but Europeans were beginning to cut down on their use of

Oil of cinnamon is used to perfume soaps, scents and cosmetics and was once an ingredient in old style pomanders. Cinnamon sticks can be added to pot-pourri.

spices, so the Dutch deliberately burnt their Amsterdam warehouses to maintain high prices. In 1772 cinnamon plants were smuggled from the Dutch plantations and used to set up areas of cultivation in the French colonies. Later, Sri Lanka was taken by the English, who dominated the cinnamon trade for many years after.

— CULTIVATION —

Cinnamon trees grow best just inland from tropical shores. The evergreen trees are frequently cropped to make them into low, dense bushes. Harvesting takes place in the rainy season. Two or three branches are taken from each tree with a special axe known as a katty. After a few hours the branches are taken to a peeling shed called a wadi. It is a large room, open on one side in which the workers sit in rows on the floor. On one side, women and children scrape away the thin, outer bark and rub the branch with brass rods to make the inner bark come away more easily. Skilled workers, usually men, on the other side of the wadi slit the bark before lifting it off with a stick.

The strips of inner bark are sun-dried which makes them curl into the familiar quills. These are then cut to a standard length, any small chips being used to fill the large quills. The quills are taken to the local cinnamon merchant to be packed and marketed.

Nothing from the tree is wasted. Leaves and twigs are used in the making of cinnamon oil and the stripped sticks are used locally for firewood.

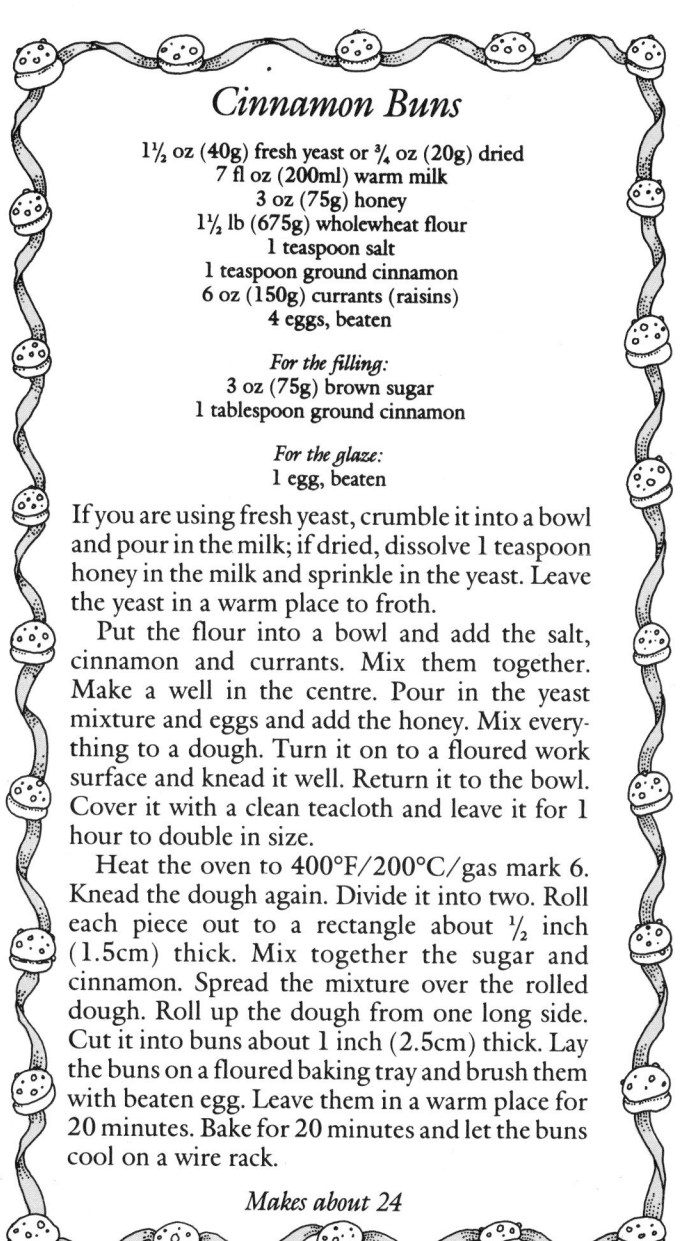

Cinnamon Buns

1½ oz (40g) fresh yeast or ¾ oz (20g) dried
7 fl oz (200ml) warm milk
3 oz (75g) honey
1½ lb (675g) wholewheat flour
1 teaspoon salt
1 teaspoon ground cinnamon
6 oz (150g) currants (raisins)
4 eggs, beaten

For the filling:
3 oz (75g) brown sugar
1 tablespoon ground cinnamon

For the glaze:
1 egg, beaten

If you are using fresh yeast, crumble it into a bowl and pour in the milk; if dried, dissolve 1 teaspoon honey in the milk and sprinkle in the yeast. Leave the yeast in a warm place to froth.

Put the flour into a bowl and add the salt, cinnamon and currants. Mix them together. Make a well in the centre. Pour in the yeast mixture and eggs and add the honey. Mix everything to a dough. Turn it on to a floured work surface and knead it well. Return it to the bowl. Cover it with a clean teacloth and leave it for 1 hour to double in size.

Heat the oven to 400°F/200°C/gas mark 6. Knead the dough again. Divide it into two. Roll each piece out to a rectangle about ½ inch (1.5cm) thick. Mix together the sugar and cinnamon. Spread the mixture over the rolled dough. Roll up the dough from one long side. Cut it into buns about 1 inch (2.5cm) thick. Lay the buns on a floured baking tray and brush them with beaten egg. Leave them in a warm place for 20 minutes. Bake for 20 minutes and let the buns cool on a wire rack.

Makes about 24

— CULINARY USES —

Although cinnamon is a sweet spice, it can be used in both sweet and savoury dishes. In medieval times it bridged the gap between sweet and savoury flavours when meat and fruit were often cooked together in pottages.

Cinnamon can be used whole or ground. Cinnamon sticks were once called 'pudding sticks' for they will readily impart their flavour when infused with milk or poached with fruit to make desserts. They can also be cooked with curries, rice or the spiced dishes of the Middle East; the sticks are removed before serving.

Add ground cinnamon to fillings for fruit pies and strudels and to sweet puddings, cakes and biscuits. Mixed with caster sugar it can be sprinkled over toast, muffins and crumpets.

Cinnamon was one of the first spices to be combined with chocolate. Try it in chocolate cakes, mousses and truffles or heat a stick with the milk for a hot chocolate drink. In Mexico, cinnamon is added to coffee and also brewed as a tea. In the eighteenth century in Scotland, a cinnamon stick was added to a pot of Indian tea. Early American colonists used cinnamon in drinks of buttered rum and in England the sticks gave flavour to hot punches and wassail bowls. Ale was once flavoured with cinnamon and now the oils of both cassia and cinnamon are used in cola drinks.

— MEDICINAL USES —

Cinnamon tea helps to check nausea and vomiting. Cinnamon oil can be used as an embrocation for rheumatism. It is also an ingredient in toothpaste and is used to flavour medicines.

— LORE —

The ancient Chinese looked on cassia as the tree of life which had flourished since the beginning of time in a beautiful garden at the source of the yellow river. Entering the garden and eating the fruit would give immortality and eternal happiness.

The legendary bird called the phoenix was said to collect cinnamon, spikenard and myrrh with which to make the magic fire from which it would be reborn.

About five hundred years before Christ, cinnamon traders spread many myths about the origins of the spice to deter others from breaking their monopoly. One story, which many people believed, was that the cinnamon sticks were used by large flesh-eating birds to make their nests. Large pieces of meat were laid out as bait which the birds subsequently took back to their nests, causing them to break under the weight so the sticks could be collected.

Cinnamon has long been regarded as an aphrodisiac, particularly in ancient Persia and later also in Europe.

I have perfumed my bed with myrrh, aloes and cinnamon. Come, let us take our fill of love until the morning; let us solace ourselves with loves.

Proverbs VII: 17–18

Cloves

E U G E N I A   C A R Y O P H Y L L U S

Cloves are one of the fragrantly sweet spices that men have fought over and risked everything to find. For many years they grew only on the Moluccan Islands, which were once called the Spice Islands and are now part of Indonesia. The Chinese were probably the first nation to import cloves and it was not until the trade centre of Constantinople was founded in 4AD that they became known in the west. Even to the Romans, they were a great luxury.

Traders in spices kept their sources of supply a secret, but in medieval times when spicy food became popular, European adventurers set out to find the plantations for themselves. Cloves were found by Marco Polo in 1298. Almost three centuries later, Magellan's expedition set out from Spain. Only one ship, the Victoria, returned, but it was loaded with cloves and nutmeg, enough spices to pay for the journey with money to spare. The captain, Sebastian del Cano was awarded a coat of arms bearing two cinnamon sticks, three nutmegs and twelve cloves. Sir Francis Drake was knighted for taking cloves to Elizabeth I of England in 1579.

In the sixteenth century, the Portuguese gained control of the Spice Islands, and they in turn were driven out by the Dutch in 1621. The Dutch guarded their monopoly jealously, destroying plantations when cloves were plentiful and too cheap. In 1772 some plants were smuggled out to the French colonies and the first crop grown outside the Moluccas was harvested four years later. From there, plants were taken to the British colonies, including India. Towards the end of the eighteenth century, the Dutch monopoly ended as Britain took most of the spice-growing areas.

The majority of the world's cloves now come from Tanzania and smaller amounts are exported from Zanzibar, Sri Lanka, Indonesia and the Malagasy Republic.

— CULTIVATION —

The clove tree is a member of the evergreen myrtle family and it is the flower buds that, when dried, become

Apple Crumble with Cloves

1lb cooking apples
½ teaspoon ground cloves
3 oz (75g) honey
4 oz (125g) wholewheat flour
3 oz (75g) brown sugar
2 oz (50g) butter

Heat the oven to 400°F/200°C/gas mark 6. Peel, core and chop the apples. Mix them with ¼ teaspoon cloves and the honey. Put them into an ovenproof dish. Put the flour, remaining cloves and sugar into a bowl and rub in the butter until the mixture resembles breadcrumbs. Sprinkle the mixture over the apples. Bake the crumble for 25 minutes or until the top is brown and crisp.

Serves 4

by hand. After three days of sun-drying they become black, having lost two thirds of their weight. The yield of each tree is about 7 lb (3.15kg) of dried cloves. It is possible to harvest two crops per year, but often only one is taken to avoid damage to the tree.

— CULINARY USES —

Cloves have both sweet and savoury uses. In medieval times they bridged the gap between sweet and sour flavours in dishes that were a mixture of meat and fruits. They also hid the flavour of tainted meat and were often used with beef or ox-tongue. The idea of sticking cloves into an onion to flavour pot-roasted meat and braised dishes came from France in the seventeenth century and this is a particularly good flavourer for beef dishes. The Romans cooked pork and ham with cloves. Add them to the pot when the meats are being boiled or stick them into the meat for roasting. Slivers of garlic and cloves give roast lamb an unusual flavour and a pinch of cloves can be added to stuffings for poultry.

Add three or four whole cloves to the pan when boiling white beans or add a pinch to nut roasts. A pinch of ground cloves is essential in a traditional British bread sauce.

In India, the clove is an ingredient in the spice mixture known as garam masala and it is also used in curries, pickles and sauces. In Western countries, both ground cloves and clove oil are added to sauces, pickles, preserves and meat products. In France *époisses* cheese is flavoured with cloves.

In the West, cloves are now mainly

the familiar, dark coloured, nail-shaped spice. They grow in clusters on the ends of the twigs, pale green at first and ripening to a red blush which indicates that they are ready for picking. If the flower buds are allowed to open, they lose their fragrance and produce oblong fruits known as 'the mother of cloves'.

Women and children pick the lower branches and men the upper ones, pulling them down with hooked poles. The complete twigs are picked from the tree and the buds are later removed

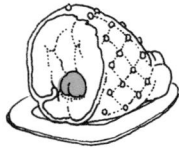

used domestically in sweet dishes. They are added whole or ground to apple pies and stuck into baked apples. Ground cloves are put into Christmas puddings, mincemeat, ginger cakes and honey cakes. They are used in cakes, confectionery and desserts in India and in Turin in Italy, whole cloves are pushed into the ends of candied walnuts.

For centuries, whole cloves have given flavour to mulled drinks and you can also add them to herb teas.

— MEDICINAL USES —

The ancient Chinese used clove oil as a mild anaesthetic for toothache, and it is still used for this purpose. It is an ingredient of digestive medicines, mouthwashes and toothpastes and was once added to health-giving toilet waters which were said to promote long life and keep away infections. In India, cloves and other whole spices are wrapped in betel nut leaves and chewed after a meal to sweeten the breath and prevent indigestion.

— SPECIAL USES —

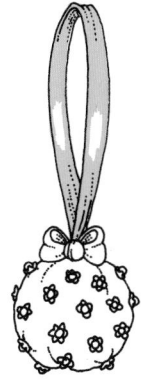

Oil of cloves is used in the making of soaps, perfumes and cosmetics. In medieval and Tudor times cloves were burnt to perfume rooms and the oil was used to scent gloves. Stuck into an orange and rubbed with orris root they make a fragrant pomander, and cloves can also be added to a pot-pourri.

In Indonesia they are mixed with tobacco and made into cigarettes called *kretek* because they crackle as they burn.

— LORE —

In the Moluccas it is said that villagers once treated blossoming clove trees like pregnant women. No man could approach them with a hat on, no noise could be made near them and no light or fire could be carried past them at night for fear that they would not bear fruit.

At the time when the Dutch were destroying clove plantations, Moluccans planted a clove tree at the births of their children, believing that if the tree flourished, so would the child.

In some Moluccan villages even today, the religious leader must be present on the first day of harvest and also when new seedlings are planted. Trees can only be planted when there is no moon and they must be shaken during an eclipse.

In third-century China officers of the court had to hold cloves in their mouths when addressing the emperor.

In ancient Persia, cloves and clove oil were used in the making of love potions and philtres.

The most beautiful, the most elegant, the most precious of all trees.

RUMPHIUS, early seventeenth-century botanist

 # *Cumin*

C U M I N U M   C Y N I N U M

The small, elongated brown cumin seeds, with their dry, slightly bitter flavour are a spice of the Middle East. They came originally from the Upper Nile but since early times have been cultivated all round the Mediterranean, and in India and China. In more recent years, Iran has been one of the most important exporters.

Cumin is mentioned in both Old and New Testaments of the Bible. Pharisees paid their tithes in cumin seed and even in medieval England, quit-rents by way of cumin seed were paid in lieu of feudal services. Cumin was one of the most common of spices grown in eastern and western Europe during the Middle Ages. Spanish explorers took it to Latin America where it is still extensively used.

For the fitches are not threshed with a threshing instrument, neither is a cart wheel turned about the cumin; but the fitches are beaten out with a staff, and the cumin with a rod.

Isaiah XXVIII, 27

— CULTIVATION —

Although cumin flourishes best in hot countries, it is possible to grow it successfully in temperate climates, although in a cool summer it may not seed. Cumin plants are very delicate members of the umbellifer family. They are best sown directly into the herb garden in spring and kept covered with cloches until midsummer. They are too fragile to transplant, so thin them out to 6 inches (15cm) within the rows and keep them well weeded. The seedheads should be cut just before they are ripe, as soon as they begin to turn brown. Hang them up with the heads encased in a paper bag in a warm, airy place.

— CULINARY USES —

Cumin, both ground and whole, features greatly in the cooking of the Middle East and of India. It is an essential ingredient of curry powder, garam masala and the Middle Eastern spice mixture known as ras-el-hanout. It can be added alone to curries, stews and casseroles and is often used to flavour rice and couscous. In India, the seeds are gently roasted before being ground to bring out the flavour. In Greece, cumin is regarded as excellent flavouring for lamb and in Holland and Switzerland the seeds are added whole to some cheeses. In France and Germany, ground cumin

Pine Nut Pilaff

2 tablespoons olive oil
1 large onion, thinly sliced
1 garlic clove, chopped
8 oz (225g) long-grain brown rice
2 teaspoons ground cumin
1 teaspoon ground turmeric
20 fl oz (575ml) stock
2 oz (50g) currants
2 oz (50g) pine nuts
4 tablespoons natural yoghurt

Heat the oil in a saucepan on a low heat. Put in the onion and garlic and soften them. Stir in the rice, cumin and turmeric. Stir for 1 minute. Pour in the stock and bring it to the boil. Cover and simmer for 30 minutes. Add the currants, cover again, and cook for 10 minutes. Take the pan from the heat. Stir in the pine nuts and yoghurt. Cover and leave to stand for 5 minutes.

Serves 4

and cumin seeds flavour bread, cakes and pastries.

In the first century BC, Celts along the Atlantic coast of France baked fish with cumin, salt and vinegar. The Romans used cumin in sauces for shellfish and dressings for lettuce. In medieval England cumin sauce was served especially with boiled chicken.

— MEDICINAL USES —

Cumin has had few medicinal uses in Europe. The Romans used it as a digestive with bread and wine, and Gerard recommended adding it to soup for chest colds. In *Bankes' Herbal* it was recommended 'to destroy wicked winds and other evils in a man's stomach'.

In India, however, the use of cumin has been more popular. It is used as a carminative, to relieve flatulence, and a digestive when made into a drink with mint, ginger, sugar, lemon juice and tamarind water. Oil of cumin dripped on to a sugar lump will calm the nerves after a shock. It can also be used as a rub for rheumatic pains and sprains.

— SPECIAL USES —

It was once thought that giving cumin seeds to poultry would keep them from straying. The seeds were also mixed with other spices, salt, flour and clay and baked into a kind of bread that was given to pigeons to keep them healthy.

— LORE —

Cumin had the reputation of being able to keep lovers faithful and so it was used in love potions and charms. At German weddings in the Middle Ages, the bride and groom carried cumin, dill and salt in their pockets. In other parts of Europe, a young soldier leaving his sweetheart would share with her a glass of wine containing ground cumin and he would carry away with him a loaf of cumin bread that she had baked.

Both Greeks and Romans, however, looked on cumin as a symbol of greed. Antonius Pius, a Roman emperor who spent little on himself, was nicknamed 'the cumin spitter'.

Ginger

Ginger is one of the so-called sweet spices and it can add its delicate and subtle flavour to dishes that are either sweet or savoury, familiar or exotic. Its origins are in the damp, tropical forests of south-east Asia and it has been used since ancient times. It was grown by the ancient Greeks and Egyptians and overland caravans from the east carried it to the Romans. To them it was the second most important spice after pepper, being used both medicinally and in spiced sauces. Because of these ancient trade routes, ginger was one of the first of the exotic spices to be used in the West. In the thirteenth century, Marco Polo discovered it growing in China and from then on plentiful supplies were able to reach Europe where it became, together with pepper, one of the cheaper spices sold by travelling pedlars at fairs.

Ginger was naturalized in America by the sixteenth century and was transplanted to Spain from the West Indies. India is now the world's largest producer of ginger, although that from Jamaica and the West Indies is said to be the best. Other exporting countries include West Africa, Japan, China, Malaysia, Vietnam, Taiwan, the Antilles and Australia.

The ginger plant resembles a tall lily with orchid-like pale yellow, purple-tipped flowers growing in a spike. The part used is the knobbly, creeping rhizome which has several 'fingers' and a rough, pale brown skin. This rhizome is sold fresh as green ginger, in whole dried pieces known as races or hands, dried and ground and also candied and crystallized.

— CULTIVATION —

Ginger needs a warm, humid climate and either heavy rainfall or constant irrigation.

The rhizomes of the ginger plant have to be at least a year old when they are harvested and they are dug after the flowers and leaves have died down. Basically, there are two commercial types of ground ginger, black and white. They are rarely labelled as such and the ground ginger that we buy is most likely to be a mixture.

To produce black ginger, the rhizomes are washed, scalded in boiling water and then sun-dried without peeling. White ginger, which has the better flavour, is produced by scraping the rhizomes but not scalding them before drying. Whole dried ginger root is produced in the same way as white ginger. It may also have an additional soaking in lime juice and water to bleach it white.

For making preserved ginger, the rhizomes are dug when they are young and green, scalded, soaked for several days in three or four changes of water and peeled, before being steeped in a syrup.

They sette hym roiall spicerye and gyngerbread.

GEOFFREY CHAUCER, fourteenth century

Ginger roots, fit for preserving, and in size equal to West Indian, have been produced in the Royal Agricultural Garden in Edinburgh.

MRS BEETON, 1861

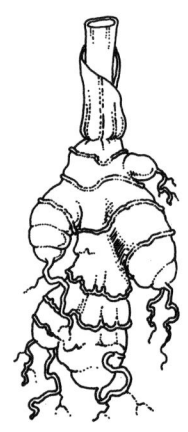

Molasses Ginger Cake

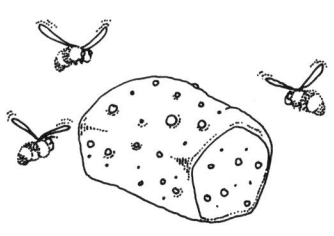
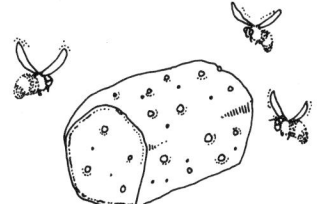

8 oz (225g) wholewheat flour
2 teaspoons ground ginger
½ teaspoon ground nutmeg
1 teaspoon baking powder
6 oz (175g) butter
3 oz (75g) brown sugar
3 oz (75g) molasses
3 eggs, beaten
4 pieces preserved ginger in syrup
3 oz (75g) sultanas

Heat the oven to 350°F/180°C/gas mark 4. Put the flour into a bowl with the spices and baking powder. Make a well in the centre. Gently melt together the butter, sugar and molasses. Cool them a little and stir them into the flour together with the eggs. Finely chop the preserved ginger.

Fold it into the mixture together with the sultanas.

Put the mixture into a greased 2 lb (900g) loaf tin and bake the cake for 1 hour or until a skewer inserted in the centre comes out clean. Turn the cake on to a wire rack to cool.

— CULINARY USES —

Being one of the cheaper, more readily available spices, ginger has been used since Norman times in a wide variety of dishes, from a sauce for seasoning beaver's tail to puddings and cakes.

Ground ginger is often added to the curries and spice mixtures of India and Sri Lanka. It is the most frequently used spice in China, being added to many dishes together with garlic, soy sauce and spring onions. It can also be used in chutneys, sauces and, in moderation, salad dressings.

Sprinkle ginger over apples or rhubarb for a pie, add a pinch to sweet pastries and crumble toppings or let its dry, hot flavour contrast superbly with fresh melon.

Fresh ginger root has to be peeled and grated before use. It is used frequently in south-east Asia and also in China.

Dried whole ginger root should be used when the flavour of ginger is required but you do not wish to spoil a clear appearance with a ground spice. Add it to syrups for fruit, mulled drinks, pickles and preserves. Bruise it with a hammer before use to bring out the flavour and discard it after cooking.

Add chopped preserved ginger to marmalade and to steamed puddings and cakes. Use it sliced to decorate

cakes and desserts and add a small amount of its syrup to fruit salads or whipped cream. In India, where it is made, the syrup left over from ginger production is fermented to make what is known as 'cool drink'. In England, fresh or dried ginger is used to make a country wine, and ginger ale and ginger beer are also popular.

The story of gingerbread is a long one. The first recipe is said to have been devised by a baker from Rhodes in ancient Greece. The Romans took it to Britain where it was baked in Anglo-Saxon monasteries before becoming a favourite Norman sweetmeat. It was often gilded or given a pattern of box leaves secured by cloves. Elizabeth I's baker shaped gingerbread in the likeness of her courtiers. Black treacle became a favourite ingredient in the seventeenth century. There have been many gingerbread recipes since then and a northern English variation is parkin. Ginger biscuits and gingerbread men were sold at fairs.

— MEDICINAL USES —

Ginger is used in Indian Ayurvedic medicine as a carminative and as a remedy for dyspepsia and flatulence. It was once thought to be an antidote to plague.

An infusion of fresh ginger root soothes colds and coughs.

— SPECIAL USES —

Oil of ginger is occasionally used in oriental perfumes and cosmetics. Whole dried ginger root can be added to pot-pourri.

Ginger is generally considered as less pungent and heating to the system than might be expected from its effects on the organs of taste, and it is frequently used, with considerable effect, as an anti-spasmodic and carminative.

MRS BEETON, 1861

Juniper

J U N I P E R U S   C O M M U N I S

Had juniper been a rare tropical spice it would probably have been far more valued, but it is an evergreen tree native to Britain and Europe, North America, North Africa and Asia. Its berries have never been much coveted and are now little used but, when crushed, they impart a mild yet richly pungent scent. Their chief claim to fame is that they are an essential ingredient in gin, and yet they blend with many dishes, both savoury and sweet. Most commercially used juniper berries are grown in Eastern Europe.

— CULTIVATION —

Juniper grows more as a shrubby bush than a tree. It is hardy and will grow well in an open situation in any soil. It can also be grown as a hedge. The berries may take up to three years to ripen completely. They are green at first and gradually become deep purple or black and it is when they reach this stage, usually in late summer, that they should be picked. Dry them on trays and store them in airtight containers.

Juniper berries retain their fleshy

Andrew Boorde in the *Dyetary of Helth*, 1542, recommended burning juniper along with rushes, rosemary, bay leaves or frankincense 'to expel all corrupt and contagious air in the, buttery, the cellar, the kitchen, the larder house. . . .'

texture even when dry, so are never sold ground. Whole berries should be crushed with a pestle and mortar before use.

— CULINARY USES —

The chief spirit of sixteenth-century Europe was brandy. The Dutch, who boasted few vineyards, began to replace it with corn spirits. Juniper soon became the chief flavourer and the drink travelled to Britain as gin. At the same time juniper was an ingredient in a distilled Elizabethan drink known as *aqua vitae* or *aqua composita*. Other distilled, juniper-flavoured drinks have included *sciedam* from Holland, *pecquet* from Liège, *Wacholderschnaps* from Westphalia and *aquavit* from Denmark in which the berries may also be combined with anise or cumin seeds. In France and also in Sweden, juniper berries are brewed with hops in the making of some beers. The Laplanders drink juniper tea.

Juniper is the perfect spice for rich meats and game. Crushed berries mixed with salt and garlic can be rubbed on to pork, game birds and lamb before cooking. Pork pâtés and stuffings for all types of game benefit from a few crushed berries. So, too, do marinades, brines and dry salting mixtures. Veal kidneys cooked with juniper and flamed in gin is a dish originating from Liège. Commercially, juniper is added to the chorizo sausages of Spain.

Juniper and cabbage are an excellent combination. Toss the crushed berries with butter into cooked cabbage or add it to sauerkraut. A savoury butter containing juniper makes a good topping for baked or boiled potatoes.

Juniper is not frequently used in sweet dishes, but it combines very well with apples.

... these are neglected in English cooking, but much appreciated in Flanders and the north of France where they are used as flavourings in dishes like partridge or pheasant braised with cabbage or choucroute.

MARCEL BOULESTIN, 1930

Spiced Beef

6 lb (2.7kg) boned brisket or flank of beef
4 teaspoons black peppercorns
4 teaspoons juniper berries
1 teaspoon allspice berries
1 teaspoon cloves
1 garlic clove, finely chopped
8 tablespoons coarse sea salt
4 tablespoons molasses

If the beef is rolled, untie it and spread it flat. Crush together the spices and garlic. Mix them with the salt and stir in the molasses. Spread the mixture over all surfaces of the beef. If the beef is in a long, thin strip, fold it in three. If the beef is thick, either fold it in two or leave it unfolded. Put it into a large, flat dish and cover it with greaseproof paper. Put it into a cool larder or room with no heat and leave it for 4 days, turning it and rubbing the brine into it every day.

Take out the beef and rinse it with cold water. Tie it securely. Bring a large pan of water to the boil and simmer the beef for 2 hours. Cool it in the liquid for 30 minutes. Cool it, with a weight on top, for 12 hours.

Serves 12 or more

— MEDICINAL USES —

Juniper was once thought to be an antidote to poison and to infection. The berries were burned in public places in times of plague and also in hospitals during the French smallpox epidemic of 1870.

An infusion of berries cures flatulence and indigestion and is also said to relieve rheumatism. Oil simmered with the berries is used as a rub for rheumatic aches. In France, the berries were chewed to relieve chest complaints, including consumption. In the sixteenth century, the berries were rubbed on the gums to ease the effects of scurvy and were added to a bath with wood ashes as a cure for itch, scabs and leprosy.

Because of its pleasant flavour, juniper is used to disguise the taste of medicines and tonics.

— HOUSEHOLD USES —

The leaves were used for strewing and were burnt to purify the air. The berries are used in toilet waters, and can be made into a light brown dye.

— LORE —

In Catholic countries there is a belief that the Holy family took refuge behind a juniper bush during the flight into Egypt. The Old Testament describes the story of Elijah being protected from the persecutions of Ahab by the juniper tree. As a result, juniper has come to be a symbol of protection against evil.

Mustard

B R A S S I C A A L B A

Mustard has always been the poor man's spice, since the time when imported exotic spices were scarce and expensive, but home-grown mustard seeds were cheap and plentiful.

Mustard has been known to man since prehistoric times. Most varieties are of Asiatic origin and have been used in China for thousands of years. The Greeks and the Romans called mustard *sinapis* and it was the Romans who took it all over Britain and Europe. When the French started to mix the pounded seeds with wine must, the name mustard was first used.

In medieval Europe, mustard was the cheapest spice of all, costing less than a farthing a pound. In one early fifteenth-century English household 84lb (38kg) were used in one year. Until the eighteenth century, mustard seeds were coarsely ground without being stripped from their husks, using small stone querns. The ground mustard was formed into balls with honey, vinegar and other spices which were crushed and mixed with water when needed.

The discovery of being able to grind mustard like wheat has been attributed to a Mrs Clements of

Durham, England, in about 1730. She took her Durham mustard by packhorse from town to town and it eventually reached the table of King George I and made her a fortune.

There are basically three species of mustard: yellow or white (*Brassica alba*), black mustard (*Brassica nigra*) and brown mustard (*Brassica juncea*). Black mustard was once the most widely cultivated but as it is difficult to harvest mechanically it is gradually being superseded by brown. Both black and brown mustard have the more pungent flavours, whereas white mustard provides a sharp hotness. Most mustard powder sold today is in the form of a fine, yellow powder, which is a combination of black or brown and yellow mustard, together with a little wheat flour and turmeric.

The past few years have seen a reviving interest in mustard. There are many different types of made mustard on the market, both coarse and smooth, mild, spicy or hot. Also, different mixes of dry mustards are available. The skill of the medieval mustard maker is at last being recognized.

— CULTIVATION —

Mustard is now grown in most temperate countries. The seed is sown in fields in the spring, yellow flowers appear in early summer, and the crop is mechanically harvested in late summer and early autumn. The seeds are graded, cleaned and dried twice and the two types of mustard seed are ground separately. In the milling machine the husk is split open and

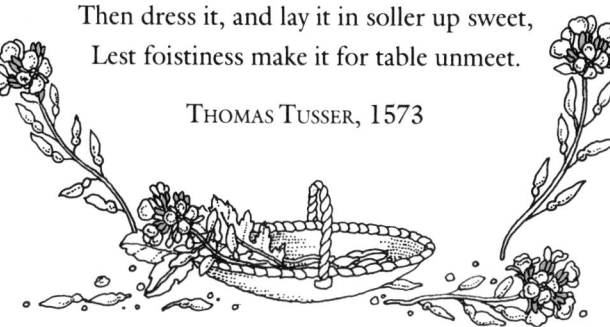

Maids, mustard-seed gather, for being too ripe,
And weather it well, ere ye give it a stripe:
Then dress it, and lay it in soller up sweet,
Lest foistiness make it for table unmeet.

THOMAS TUSSER, 1573

separated from the kernel which is then ground on rollers and sieved. The different colours of mustard powder being used are then blended together. The husk is used to make mustard oil in both edible and non-edible grades.

— CULINARY USES —

Mustard has been used as a condiment with meats since Roman times and probably before. The Romans ate it with sausage and wild boar; in medieval times it was essential accompaniment for the brawn that was served on festive occasions and in later years in English cottages, a creamy mustard sauce was served with the more homely pig's-head brawn. Herbs, spices, honey, milk, wine and vinegar and other ingredients including ground nuts have all been mixed with the ground mustard seeds to make

Good Master Mustardseed, I know your patience well: that same cowardly, giant-like ox-beef hath devoured many a gentleman of your house: I promise you your kindred hath made my eyes water ere now.

WILLIAM SHAKESPEARE,
A Midsummer Night's Dream

The great art of mixing mustard is to have it perfectly smooth, and of a proper consistency.

ELIZA ACTON, 1845

Pork Chops with Onion and Mustard Sauce

4 pork chops
1 large onion, quartered and thinly sliced
3½ fl oz (100ml) milk
sea salt and freshly ground black pepper
4 tablespoons mustard powder
1 teaspoon white mustard seeds
6 sage leaves, chopped

Heat the oven to 400°F/200°C/gas mark 6. Put the onion into a saucepan with the milk. Bring it to the boil and simmer for 2 minutes. Put the mustard powder, mustard seeds and sage into a bowl. Stir in the milk and onions.

Cut the rind from the chops. Coat one side of the chops with a thin layer of the sauce. Put them on a rack in a roasting tin, coated side down. Coat the upper side with the remaining sauce. Put the chops into the oven for 45 minutes, until cooked.

Serves 4

accompaniments for different dishes.

To make up mustard powder, simply mix it to a paste with a little tepid water and leave it to stand for 15 minutes for the flavours to develop. Vinegar, salt or boiling water added directly to the powder may produce a bitter flavour. If a sharper flavour is wanted, add a little vinegar before serving.

Mustard powder can be added with the flour when making a white sauce and provides seasoning for savoury breads, scones, dumplings, pancakes and fritters. A little added to a salad dressing will help to stabilize the emulsion; a small amount is essential in the making of mayonnaise. Braised vegetables such as celery or turnips can be flavoured with mustard pow-der, so too can soups such as onion or potato. After cooking, the dish is left with a mustard flavour but not hotness. Herrings and mackerel can be sprinkled with mustard before grilling or given a coating of oatmeal or flour seasoned with mustard.

Made mustard can also be added to sauces, soups and salad dressings, but only sparingly since the hotness is preserved. Bought spiced mustards can be used in the same ways. They can also be spread over chops and steaks before grilling or added to casseroles and stews; the milder types can be used with white fish.

Whole mustard seeds are mostly used to flavour pickling vinegars. Coarsely ground, they can be added to marinades, sauces and sauté dishes.

— MEDICINAL USES —

Both white and black mustard seeds have been used medicinally. They have similar properties but the black has been considered the most effective.

A poultice of black mustard seeds laid on the chest relieves congestion in cases of chest cold, bronchitis and pneumonia. The same poultice will also relieve neuralgia. The crushed seeds in a bowl of boiling water make a warming and stimulating foot bath that has long been used to cure colds and headaches. A little black mustard powder in hot water is said to relieve hiccoughs. Culpeper recommended that the seeds be chewed to soothe toothache and that a decoction of the seeds should be administered to counteract mushroom poisoning.

Mustard oil produced from the hulls of the seeds only makes a good rub for rheumatic pains. Oil produced from the whole seeds must first be mixed with spirit of camphor.

White mustard has been recommended for digestive disorders. An infusion of the crushed seeds can be drunk to ease bronchitis or used as a gargle for a sore throat.

— SPECIAL USES —

Mustard has been grown as a fodder crop for sheep and also as green manure to enrich the soil. If ploughed in while still in flower it will help rid the soil of insect pests.

Nutmeg and Mace

MYRISTICA FRAGRANS 'HOUTT'

The fruit of the nutmeg tree provides two sweet spices in one. When the small round fruits ripen the thick outer coat splits to reveal a bright red filigree jacket clasped around a shiny, dark brown shell. The red jacket is dried to become mace, while inside the shell is the small, oval nutmeg.

Nutmeg originally came from the tiny Indonesian islands called the Moluccas, or the Spice Islands. It first reached the West via the old trade routes when Constantinople was founded in the fourth century, and by the twelfth century was in great demand.

Marco Polo found nutmeg growing in the Far East in 1298 and from that time on Portugal had a monopoly over the spice trade. The Moluccans were plundered by Magellan's ships in 1522 and in the seventeenth century fell to the Dutch, who then completely controlled the nutmeg market. Their monopoly was eventually broken by the French and English who set up plantations in their own colonies, including Penang and the West Indies. In 1843 nutmegs were first grown in Grenada, which came to be known as the Nutmeg Isle and which still exports thirty per cent of the world's crop. The rest comes from Indonesia.

Nutmeg has always been highly

valued in Europe for both culinary and medicinal use. Cooks and apothecaries in medieval England, unless very careful, might well find they had been sold a carved wooden imitation. In the eighteenth century special nutmeg graters were made, out of any material from tin to silver and ivory, which folded and contained a single nut. They were carried by men in waistcoat pockets and by ladies on a small chain, to be used for both mulled ale and medicaments.

— CULTIVATION —

The nutmeg tree thrives on tropical islands near the sea about 1000 feet (300 metres) above sea level. It is an evergreen with shiny leaves similar to those of the bay tree, taking up to twenty years to mature and bear fruit, but productive for up to forty years after maturing.

The fruits are harvested using a long pole with a basket on the end, which in Indonesia is called a gai-gai. First the outer husk is stripped away with a large knife and then the mace is carefully removed. It is pressed between boards and sun-dried, but remains crimson until it is packed and is in transit to market. Grenadan mace is cured before packing by storing it in the dark for up to three months, a process which makes it light tan and very brittle. Mace can be exported whole or ground.

After the mace has been removed the nutmegs are sun-dried in their shells for one week until they rattle. The shells are broken with a hammer and the nutmegs removed. Like mace, they are exported whole or ground.

— CULINARY USES —

Both mace and nutmeg have always had both sweet and savoury uses. Mace has been favoured in England for use in potted meats and fish, sauces and stuffings and bread sauce. Commercially, it is used in sausages, frankfurters and meat loaf. It has a mild, bitter-sweet flavour and is good with the milder meats such as veal, chicken and turkey and also with fish. Add a blade of mace when poaching smoked fish in milk or when baking white fish. Infuse it in the milk with which you are going to make a soufflé. Mace is the traditional spice used in Pound Cake, in both Britain and America. Add it also to cherry pie, chocolate dishes and whipped, sweetened cream. It is best to keep both whole and ground mace in the spice cupboard.

The third course was rabbits in gravy, and meat cooked in Cyprus wine, with mace, cubebs and cloves, washed down with quantities of red and white wine.

WALTER DE
BIBBESWORTH,
thirteenth century

With nutmegs too, to put in ale
No matter whether fresh or stale,
Or else to keep in coffer.

GEOFFREY CHAUCER, fourteenth century

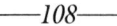

Christmas Pudding

2 oz (50g) currants
3 oz (75g) raisins
3 oz (75g) sultanas
2 oz (50g) candied peel, chopped
2 oz (50g) stoned dates, chopped
7 fl oz (200ml) brandy
1½ oz (40g) wholewheat breadcrumbs
1½ oz (40g) wholewheat flour
2 oz (50g) beef suet
½ teaspoon baking powder
pinch of sea salt
½ nutmeg, grated
½ teaspoon ground cinnamon
1 medium carrot
1 small cooking apple
1 oz (25g) flaked almonds
1 egg, beaten
butter, for greasing pudding basin

Put the currants, raisins, sultanas, candied peel and dates into a bowl. Pour in 5 fl oz (150ml) brandy and leave to soak overnight.

Grease a 30 fl oz (850ml) pudding basin with butter. Put the breadcrumbs, flour, suet, baking powder, salt and spices into a mixing bowl. Grate in the carrot and the apple. Crumble in the almonds. Mix in the fruits together with their brandy. Mix in the egg and remaining brandy.

Put the mixture into the prepared basin. Cover with a layer of buttered greaseproof paper and one of foil, each with a pleat in the centre. Tie down with string. Bring a pan of water to the boil. Lower in the pudding and steam it for 4 hours. Cool it and change the paper and foil. Steam for a further 2 hours before serving.

Serves 8

Nutmeg is best bought whole and grated when needed. The flavour of ready-ground nutmeg is much dulled and deteriorates with age. Grate nutmeg into pudding, cake and biscuit mixtures, into fruit pies and over custard tarts and trifles. It is excellent with cheese and egg dishes, with vegetables such as spinach and cabbage, and in creamy-textured soups. In Scandinavia it is added to meat balls and in Germany to potato dumplings.

In the eighteenth century, nutmeg was grated into mulled ale and wine and even before that nutmeg chips were added to freshly barrelled ale to sharpen the flavour. Nutmeg oil is now one of the ingredients in cola drinks.

— MEDICINAL USES —

Both nutmeg and mace have been highly valued medicinally but their present uses are few. Nutmeg sprinkled into drinks is said to be good for convalescents and helps to relieve nausea caused by other drugs. In India, mace is chewed for bad breath. In the nineteenth century, nutmeg tea was a remedy for insomnia.

Nutmeg was once believed to combat plague and was made into vinegars and cordial waters for that purpose.

— COSMETIC USES —

In the sixteenth century, nutmeg was used as a perfume for gloves and was an ingredient in the early type of pomanders. The oil is now used in soaps, perfumes and hair lotions.

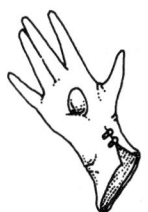

Paprika

C A P S I C U M   A N N U M

Paprika is a warm, red spice with a mild, aromatic, bitter-sweet flavour. Compared to some, it is a relatively new spice, being one of the many varieties of *Capsicum* found by Christopher Columbus in Central America in 1493 and taken back to be grown around the Mediterranean. The fiery flavour of many peppers is due to a substance called capsaicin. When they were grown in Europe, the capsaicin content lessened to produce the milder variety known as *Capsicum annum*. After reaching Spain the plants travelled to Morocco and other Islamic countries, including Turkey, and the soldiers of the Sultan carried it with them when they conquered Hungary in 1699. It has since become a feature of much Eastern European cooking. *Capsicum annum* was also found in the nineteenth century growing wild in India, Abyssinia and Central Africa.

Paprika was once fed to canaries to give them a good colour.

— CULTIVATION —

Paprika is now mainly produced in Central Europe and Spain. A small amount is also grown in California for use in the United States.

The two main paprika towns of Hungary are Szeged and Kalocsa, both located in the south of the country where the springs are warm and damp and the summers hot and dry. *Capsicum annum* is grown as an annual and its cone-shaped pods are harvested in late summer when they are 3–5 inches (7.5–12.5cm) long and hanging downwards from the stems. On the state-owned plantations, the pods are dried and crushed by machine, but there are still some families who thread the pods on to strings, hang them on the eaves to dry and crush them with an implement known as a kulu. This is said to produce the best flavoured paprika.

Paprika from Hungary generally has a stronger flavour than that from Spain.

— CULINARY USES —

Paprika, lard and soured cream form the basis of Hungarian cooking. Together they flavour the four hearty meat dishes, gulyas, porkolt, paprikas and tokany.

Paprika is a favourite spice in Spain and Portugal where it is added to garlic soup, white fish and shellfish,

Spanish Omelette

5 oz (150g) cooked potatoes (not mashed)
4 oz (125g) chorizo sausage
1 oz (25g) lard
2 tablespoons olive oil
1 large onion, quartered and thinly sliced
1 garlic clove, finely chopped
1 teaspoon paprika
pinch of cayenne pepper
6 eggs
4 tablespoons chopped parsley

Finely chop the potatoes and chorizo sausage. Melt the lard with the oil in an omelette pan on a medium heat. Mix in the potatoes, chorizo, onion, garlic, paprika and cayenne pepper. Cook until the onion is soft, stirring frequently. Beat the eggs with the parsley and heat the grill to the highest temperature. Pour the eggs into the pan and cook them, tipping the pan and lifting the edges of the setting omelette with a knife so as much liquid egg as possible reaches the sides and base of the pan.

When the underside is brown, after about 4 minutes, put the pan under the grill and cook the omelette until it is set through, risen and golden.

Serves 4

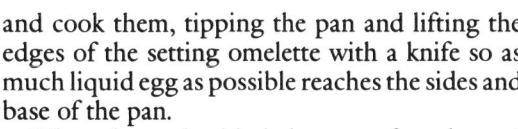

fricassees of lamb, chicken casseroles and paella. It is an essential ingredient in the rich, red-brown chorizo sausages which are added to many local dishes. Paprika can also be found in spiced Middle Eastern sauces and stews, in Indian curry mixtures and scattered over Italian pizzas.

Use it to flavour dried beans and dishes of mixed vegetables, and also in salad dressings.

Never overheat paprika, otherwise its sugar content will caramelize and the dish becomes dark brown and bitter in flavour. When adding paprika to softening onion, do so on a very low heat and put it in casseroles, stews and soups at the beginning of the cooking time.

— MEDICINAL USES —

Paprika has few medicinal uses, but is thought to stimulate the appetite and increase the flow of gastric juices. It is rich in vitamin C, one tablespoon containing as much as the juice of four lemons. It is also high in vitamins A, B1 and 2, and vitamin P.

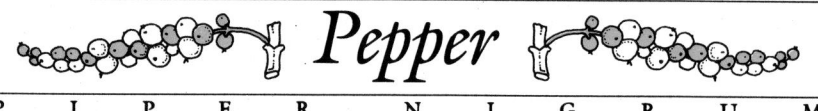

Pepper

P I P E R N I G R U M

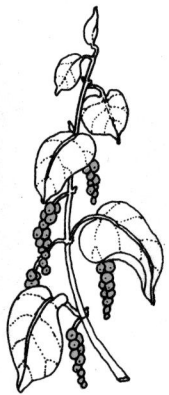

Pepper is probably the most used and abused spice in the western world; the ever present pepper pot or mill beside the stove or on the table lead it to be sprinkled over or into any dish without particular thought for the resulting flavour. Yet pepper can subtly change a dish and should in most cases be used with more care. In India it is the 'King of Spices' and others call it the 'Master Spice'.

Pepper has always been popular and relatively cheap. The Romans loved it, putting it into almost every dish they ever made, both sweet and savoury. They had it imported from the coast of Malabar and kept it in specially built warehouses. The Vandals, who were later to destroy the Roman Empire, also loved pepper. In 408AD Alaric the Visigoth was offered a huge weight of pepper, together with gold and silver, as an inducement to raise the blockade on Rome. He took his payment, and also took the city.

In Anglo-Saxon England, pepper was available only to kings, nobles and monks. It was one of the valued gifts that Bede left to his fellow monks; and in 982, in order to obtain sufficient supplies for the royal household, King Aethelred made a charge of ten pounds of pepper on any German ship coming into London to trade.

In the eleventh century, Venetian merchants began trading with the Arabs and soon pepper became available to the poorest manorial lord and a pepper horn was commonplace in the English farmhouse. The Guild of Pepperers, responsible for marketing the spice in London, was first mentioned in 1180. During the Middle Ages, the best pepper could always be bought in London, and often rich householders would send a representative to buy it for them. Inferior quality pepper was sold very cheaply at local fairs. Rents were often paid in pepper, hence the English expression 'a peppercorn rent', which means a very low or nominal rent.

In the fifteenth century the Venetian merchants decreed that all spices coming from the East had to pass through their port and that they would act as brokers. The Portuguese took over from the Venetians and later the Dutch attempted to take over from

I speak severely to my boy,
I beat him when he sneezes,
For he can thoroughly enjoy
The pepper when he pleases.

LEWIS CARROL, *Alice in Wonderland*

It is generally employed as a condiment; but it should never be forgotten that, even in small quantities, it produces detrimental effects on inflammatory constitutions.

MRS BEETON, 1861

them: all this rapidly forced up the price of pepper, causing the East India company to be formed in 1599 to protect British interests. Since then, pepper has always been one of the cheapest and most available of spices.

— CULTIVATION —

Pepper is native to Malabar on the southern part of India's east coast and it will grow only in hot jungle areas no more than 20 degrees from the equator. It is still cultivated in India but the main exporting countries are now Indonesia, Malaysia, Sri Lanka and Brazil.

Pepper is a vine plant which climbs up jungle trees. The small berries grow in long clusters and to harvest them the pickers climb up ladders made from thick bamboo poles with steps on either side. The berries are stripped by hand from the stalks and sun-dried on bamboo mats.

To produce black pepper, the berries are picked while they are still green and dried in the sun or sometimes in kilns to make them black and hard but not crumbly.

For white peppercorns, the berries are picked when they have turned red. Before drying, they are soaked in salt water to remove the outer skin.

Green peppercorns are also now available in the West. These are picked when they are unripe and are not removed from the stalks. They are tinned or pickled for export.

— CULINARY USES —

Pepper should ideally be bought whole as the flavour deteriorates consider-

Peppered Pineapple Ice-Cream

1 large pineapple
2 egg yolks
3 tablespoons honey
10 fl oz (275ml) thick cream
10 fl oz (275ml) Greek-style natural yoghurt
½ teaspoon freshly ground black pepper

Remove the husk and core from the pineapple. Reserve half and chop and liquidize the other half.

Beat the egg yolks with the honey until they are light and frothy. Heat the cream to just below boiling point. Whip it into the egg yolks. Whip in the yoghurt, followed by the liquidized pineapple and the pepper.

Chill the mixture. Put it into a freezing tray and then into the coldest part of the freezer, or into the ice compartment of the refrigerator set at the lowest temperature, for 2 hours or until it is frozen to a slush. Transfer it to a bowl and whip it to break up the ice particles. Put into a rigid plastic container, cover and freeze for a further 4 hours or until set completely.

The ice-cream should be kept in the freezer or ice compartment, now at normal temperature, for 12 hours before serving.

Before serving, move the ice-cream into the main part of the refrigerator for 30 minutes. Scoop it on to plates and garnish it with the remaining pineapple, either chopped or in segments.

Serves 6–8

ably when it is ground. Keep white pepper and black pepper in separate mills and use them in different dishes.

Black pepper is strongly aromatic besides being hot and can be used in both sweet and savoury dishes. Add whole peppercorns to stock, to court bouillon for fish and to boiled pork, salt beef and ham. Coarsely crushed they can be added to brines and dry spicing mixtures, and can be pressed into steaks before grilling. They will also add flavour to beef and pork stews and sauté dishes. Freshly milled black pepper is suitable for most casseroles and stews, vegetarian dishes and pasta. Used as a sweet spice it can be added to spiced cakes, particularly gingerbread, and also to cream and fruit desserts.

White pepper has a clean, sharp flavour and is hotter than black. It compliments most vegetables, creamy soups and fish and should always be used in pale-coloured sauces, dressings and mayonnaise, for both flavour and appearance.

Green peppercorns are generally used to make a sauce for rich poultry and game, but they are being increasingly used in other meat dishes.

— MEDICINAL USES —

When pepper is used at all medicinally it is as a digestive, to promote appetite and aid in the digestion of rich foods.

Saffron

C R O C U S   S A T I V U S

There is a legend that an early pilgrim first smuggled a saffron bulb into England by hiding it in his palmer's and '. . . with venture of his life; for if he had been taken, by the law of the country from whence it came, he had died for the fact.'

Exotic and expensive since it was first used, saffron is made up of the tiny orange-red stigmas of the saffron crocus. This is a beautiful large, purple, lily-shaped crocus with a pink-tinged stem and leaves that could be mistaken for grass. It is thought to have been originally cultivated in Cicilia, in the southern part of what is now Turkey, around the town of Corycus. But since the Middle Ages, the best saffron has come from Spain.

Saffron is mentioned in the Song of Solomon and was loved by the Phoenicians, who carried it along the Mediterranean coast to France. There is a story that they also took it to Cornwall and traded it for tin, so starting the Cornish love of saffron cake.

Both the Greeks and Romans knew saffron, calling it respectively *krokos* and *karkom*, and the Roman supplies came from around the shores of the Mediterranean. The Romans took saffron to northern Europe and to Britain.

Saffron was also much enjoyed in the Middle East. It spread first from Persia to India; and in 900AD the Arabs, who called it *zahafaran*, took it to Valencia. Rice was introduced to that part of Spain at the same time, and so began the famous paella.

Saffron was first taken to the United States by a German called Schwen-

In Porthleven in Cornwall at St Peterstide which is the end of June, the children of Methodist Churches in the area march with bands to the sea wall, through the town and up to a common, where they are each given a saffron cake.

Saffron Cake

good pinch of saffron
2 tablespoons hot water
1oz (25g) fresh yeast or ½oz (15g) dried
1 teaspoon sugar
5 fl oz (150ml) warm water
1 lb (450g) 85% wholemeal flour
pinch of fine sea salt
¼ nutmeg, grated
3 oz (75g) butter
2 oz (50g) lard
8 oz (225g) currants
1 oz (25g) candied peel, finely chopped
5 fl oz (150ml) milk

Infuse the saffron with the hot water in a covered jar overnight. Strain off and reserve the water.

If using fresh yeast, crumble it into a bowl and pour on the warm water; if dried yeast, dissolve the sugar in the water first, sprinkle in the yeast and stir. Leave the yeast in a warm place to froth.

Put the flour and salt into a bowl. Add the nutmeg. Rub in the butter and lard. Toss in the currants and candied peel. Add the saffron water to the yeast mixture. Pour it into the flour. Add the milk. Mix everything to a dough.

Knead the mixture in the bowl, taking sides to middle. Cover the bowl with a clean teacloth and leave it in a warm place for 1 hour, or until the dough has doubled in size.

Heat the oven to 350F/180C/gas mark 4. Knead the dough again. Divide it into two, and put each half into a 11b (450g) loaf tin greased with butter; or make 16 small round buns and place them on a baking sheet. Cover with a cloth and leave in a warm place for 10 minutes, or until the loaves have risen above the sides of the tins, or the buns have doubled in size.

Bake the large loaves for 1 hour; the buns for 30 minutes. Cool them on wire racks. Serve with butter.

felder, who grew it on a fairly large scale in Pennsylvania. In America, saffron cake is called Golden Schwenfelder Cake.

— CULTIVATION —

The best saffron comes from the plains of La Mancha in Spain, where it is grown on family farms and smallholdings. The corms are planted in July and the flowers gathered in September. In the evenings, the whole family sits around the table removing the brightly coloured stigmas and part of the style by hand. These are dried in a kiln between layers of thick paper and then pressed to form flat cakes. It takes sixty thousand saffron flowers to produce one pound (450g) of marketable saffron.

Always buy saffron strands rather than the powder, which will colour but not flavour and which may also have been adulterated with another spice, such as turmeric.

— CULINARY USES —

When saffron was at its most popular, it was prized most of all for its colour: '. . . and for yellow you may dye it with saffron, as yellow as you would have it.' Brawn-type dishes of both meat and fish, pottages, batters, herb sauces for fresh meat and bacon, and dishes of cabbage were all the more appreciated if they were saffron yellow. There were also some delicious sweet recipes, such as deep-fried biscuits made with honey, wine and spices, and Cawdelle Ferry, consisting of a thick mixture of egg yolks, wine, almond milk, sugar, spices and dried fruits, thickened with rice flour to the consistency of a blancmange.

Many countries of the world have special recipes using saffron. There is the Spanish paella, the French bouillabaisse and the Italian risotto. From northern India there is saffron rice and from Iran a yellow rice pudding called sholezard. Jewish cookery boasts challah, a plaited bread, and gilderne, a chicken soup made for Sabbaths, holidays and weddings.

— MEDICINAL USES —

Saffron was used medicinally in Ancient Egypt and in Greece. For many centuries it has been used in Europe to relieve nervous complaints.

In the seventeenth century it was recommended by every medical writer to 'relieve mind, body and estate'. At this time it became one of the ingredients of laudanum pills.

Saffron tea flavoured with brandy was once given for measles and saffron cordial for smallpox. The same treatment was applied to consumption.

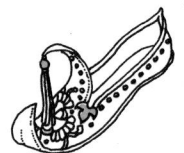

Turmeric

C   U   R   C   U   M   A   L   O   N   G   A

Warm yellow turmeric is lightly aromatic, turning any food to which it is added a beautiful golden yellow. It is not simply a cheap substitute for saffron, but has an aroma and flavour of its own.

Turmeric is related to ginger and came originally from Indonesia and China. It has been grown in India for thousands of years and in medieval times was called Indian Saffron or *Crocus indicus*. In biblical times it was used both as a perfume and as a spice and it is a favourite spice in Morocco.

— CULTIVATION —

Turmeric is now grown in China, India, the Caribbean, Java and Peru. The knobbly rhizomes are first boiled and then peeled to reveal their bright orange flesh. They are sun-dried for ten to fifteen days until they are dry and hard and produce a metallic sound when broken. They are then cleaned and polished in a motor-driven drum.

In India, some turmeric is still hand ground by professional women spice-grinders. The pieces are pounded

with a pestle and mortar and then ground to a powder with a stone known as a chakki. This turmeric is mainly sold locally in shops and street markets. Turmeric for export is stone ground in mechanical mills that each handle two tons of the spice in one day. Small amounts of turmeric are exported whole.

— CULINARY USES —

Turmeric has until recently been little used in the West although it has been known in Europe for centuries.

In India it is both colouring and flavouring for curries and rice dishes. Fish soups and fish dishes with creamy sauces benefit from a pinch of turmeric. It also goes well with chicken and can be added to savoury butters and to vegetarian dishes.

In the West, turmeric is used in pickles, particularly piccalilli, and a small proportion is added to mustard powder for its colour.

In India fruit drinks, cakes, jellies and confectionery are all coloured with turmeric. Commercially, it is added to foods such as cheese and margarine, to improve the colour and flavour and also because it is a natural anti-oxidant.

— MEDICINAL USES —

Turmeric is mainly used medicinally in India. The juice or fresh grated root is used to treat skin infections and also made into a paste with other substances to treat smallpox. An infusion is inhaled in cases of sore throat or common cold and a decoction in warm milk is drunk for the same purpose. Turmeric is an ingredient of treatments for diabetes and leprosy and is also used as a digestive. The burnt spice makes a useful tooth powder.

In medieval England, where it was a custom to treat like with like, turmeric was thought to be a cure for yellow jaundice.

In India turmeric is frequently used as a dye for cottons and silks and is also used to colour paints and varnishes. Hindus use it as a dye for ceremonial robes.

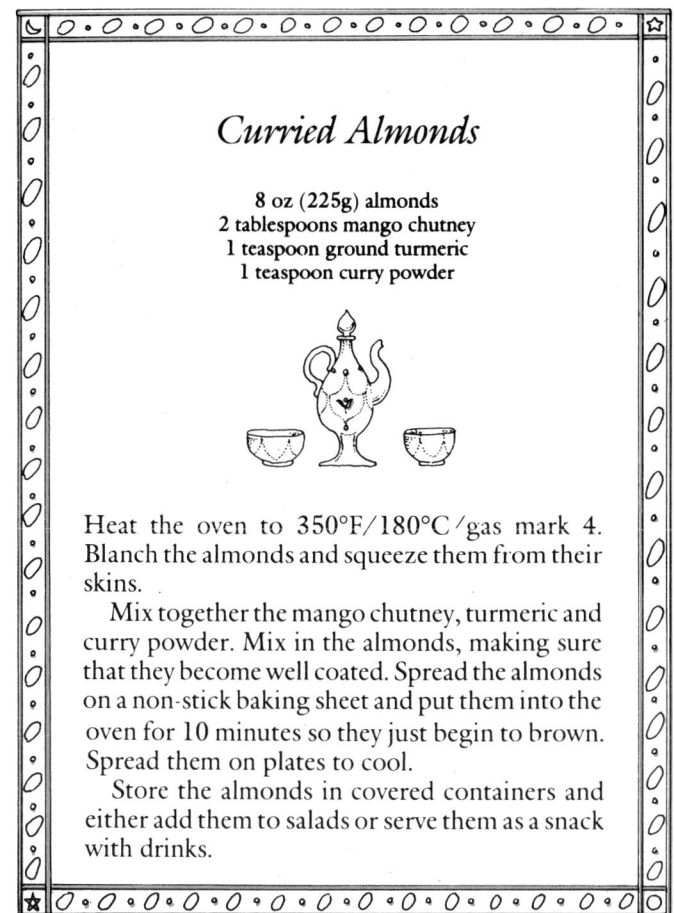

Curried Almonds

8 oz (225g) almonds
2 tablespoons mango chutney
1 teaspoon ground turmeric
1 teaspoon curry powder

Heat the oven to 350°F/180°C/gas mark 4. Blanch the almonds and squeeze them from their skins.

Mix together the mango chutney, turmeric and curry powder. Mix in the almonds, making sure that they become well coated. Spread the almonds on a non-stick baking sheet and put them into the oven for 10 minutes so they just begin to brown. Spread them on plates to cool.

Store the almonds in covered containers and either add them to salads or serve them as a snack with drinks.

— COSMETIC USES —

Cosmetics made with turmeric give the dark skins of Indian women a golden glow and in many parts of Asia turmeric water is simply used as a wash for hands and face. Face packs made from turmeric are used to cleanse and beautify the skin and discourage unwanted facial hair.

— LORE —

In many parts of India, turmeric is a spice that will bring good luck. Pieces of root were once hung round the neck of a newborn baby, or turmeric water was dabbed regularly on his head until he could walk.

In Bengal, turmeric root is burned to drive away evil spirits and ghosts.

Vanilla

VANILLA PLANIFOLIA

The soft and full, yet delicate scent of vanilla is reminiscent of orchids on a warm day and it is indeed a member of the orchid family.

Vanilla is a native of the Atlantic coast of South America and was discovered by the Spaniards in Mexico in the sixteenth century. When taken back home with them, it was described by the physician to King Philip as 'that smell of musk and balsam from New Spain'. For three hundred years after that, vanilla grew only in South America. In the nineteenth century the secret of artificial pollination was discovered, allowing it to be cultivated in other tropical and sub-tropical countries.

— CULTIVATION —

Only a small amount of the world's crop of vanilla now comes from South America. About eighty per cent is grown in the Malagasy Republic and the neighbouring Islands of Reunion and Comores. Small amounts are grown in Java, Tahiti and India.

Vanilla plants are trained up trees and posts. Their orchid-like flowers are followed by long yellow-green pods which are picked when they are unripe and have little or no scent. To cure the pods and develop the aroma they are first plunged into boiling water and while still damp are packed tightly into tins and allowed to sweat. They eventually turn dark brown and become sweetly scented and coated with a crystalline substance known as vanillin. They are then graded according to length, aroma, colour, flexibility and freedom from blemishes, insects and mildew. The highest grade, called fine vanilla, should be long and dark in colour, well coated with frosting, glossy and flexible with a strong fragrance.

Most vanilla pods are exported to Europe. For the United States, vanilla essence or extract is produced by extracting the vanilla flavour with alcohol in the presence of glycerine.

Its properties are stimulating and exciting. It is in daily use for ices, chocolates, and flavouring confections generally.

MRS BEETON, 1861

The Marquis de Frangipani, an Italian perfume maker, scented handkerchiefs and gloves with vanilla and bitter almonds. Bruised vanilla pods can be added to pot-pourri.

Plums with Rich Vanilla Custard

1lb (450g) plums
1 vanilla pod
4 tablespoons sweet sherry
3 oz (75g) demerara or coarse sugar
6 fl oz (175ml) milk
5 fl oz (150ml) thick cream
3 egg yolks

Heat the oven to 400°F/200°C/gas mark 6. Halve and stone the plums. Put them into an ovenproof dish with the sherry, 2 oz (50g) sugar and the vanilla pod. Cover them with foil and bake them for 20 minutes. Let them cool completely.

Rinse and dry the vanilla pod. Put it into a saucepan with the milk and cream. Bring to just below boiling point. Take them from the heat and remove the vanilla pod. Beat the eggs. Beat in about 3 fl oz (90ml) of the hot liquid. Stir the mixture back into the saucepan. Stir on a very low heat, without boiling, until the mixture thickens. Pour the custard into a bowl, cover it with wet greaseproof paper and allow to cool completely.

Cover the plums with the custard. Sprinkle the remaining sugar over the top. Heat a grill to the highest temperature. Put the dish under the grill until the sugar has melted and browned. Serve immediately to give a hot and cold effect.

Serves 4

— CULINARY USES —

The Aztecs used vanilla to flavour a cocoa drink which they called Xoco-Latl. A vanilla pod infused in milk for hot chocolate still makes a delicious drink. It can also be steeped in wine for making Sangria.

It was the French who first used vanilla to flavour cream, ice-cream, sherbets and sweet custard sauces. Rice puddings, mousses and cold soufflés and crème caramel can also be flavoured with a vanilla pod. Gently infuse a whole pod in the milk or cream that you intend to use for the recipe. You can also put a pod in with poaching fruit and into syrups for fruit salads. When the flavour is right, remove the vanilla pod, rinse it in cold water and return it to an air-tight container. Depending on the frequency of use, it will keep well for up to four months.

Savoury uses for vanilla are rare, but in France the seeds are grated sparingly into a mixture of spices to flavour a chicken and into a stuffing for fresh-water fish. In Denmark a vanilla-flavoured rhubarb sauce is sometimes served with braised chicken.

— MEDICINAL USES —

Vanilla was once used to treat hysterical conditions and fever and it was also believed to be a brain tonic.

Index of Recipes

Index of Ingredients

alecost leaves 16
allspice berries 63, 73, 83, 91, 103
almonds 117
almonds, flaked 109
almonds, ground 20
anchovy fillets 51
angelica, candied 18, 71
angelica leaves 18, 45
apples, Bramley 83
apples, cooking 96, 109
asparagus 57
aubergines 54

baking powder 101, 109
basil 20
bay leaves 22, 63, 69
beef, boned brisket or flank 103
beef, skirt 51
bergamot leaves 24
bitter beer 34, 67
blackcurrants 71
borage leaves 26
brandy 83, 109
breadcrumbs, wholewheat 63, 109
brewers' yeast 16
broad beans 67
butter 22, 40, 51, 67, 69, 76, 85, 96, 101, 109, 115

candied peel 109, 115
caraway seeds 85
cardamom pods 87
carrots 47, 109
cashew nuts 78
cayenne pepper 36, 89, 111
chamomile 28
cheese, Cheddar 49
cheese, Cheshire 67

cheese, Double Gloucester 32
cheese, soft 20
chervil 30
chicken 76
chickpeas 43
chillies 91
chives 32
chocolate flake 87
chorizo sausage 111
cider, dry 76
cinnamon, ground 93, 109
cinnamon stick 91
cloves 91, 96, 103
coffee, instant 87
comfrey leaves 34
coriander 36
cottage cheese 32
courgettes 49
cream of tartar 16
cream, soured 65, 79
cream, thick 18, 45, 71, 81, 113, 119
cucumber 38, 76
cumin, ground 36, 54, 99
currants 93, 99, 109, 115
curry powder 117

dates, stoned 109
dill, sprigs 38
duck 83

egg 32, 34, 57, 93, 101, 109, 111
egg plant 54
egg yolk 18, 32, 34, 81, 113, 119

fennel, chopped 40
flour, 85% 115
flour, wholewheat 32, 34, 40, 57, 71, 83, 85, 93, 96, 101, 109

French beans 78

garlic 20, 36, 43, 54, 60, 73, 78, 103, 111
gelatin 45
ginger ale 26
ginger, ground 101
ginger, preserved 101
glace cherries 45, 71
grape juice, red 18

haricot beans 69
honey 18, 24, 45, 71, 81, 85, 93, 96, 113

juniper berries 63, 73, 103

lamb 36, 60
lard 111, 115
lemon 16, 30, 40, 43
lemon balm 45
lemon juice 30, 34, 36
lemon rind 51, 76
lemon thyme 51
lettuce 76
lime, juice and rind 89
lovage 47

mackerel 30
mango chutney 117
marigold petals 49
marjoram 51
mayonnaise 47, 76
milk 18, 32, 63, 85, 87, 93, 106, 115, 119
mint 54, 89
molasses 101, 103
mustard, Dijon 47
mustard powder 30, 65, 106
mustard seeds, white 106

nutmeg, grated 109, 115
nutmeg, ground 101

olive oil 20, 30, 36, 43, 60, 65, 89, 99, 111
onion 20, 36, 51, 63, 67, 69, 83, 99, 106, 111
oranges 24
orange slices 28
orange juice 26, 28

paprika 36, 111
parsley 32, 34, 38, 43, 49, 51, 57, 69, 89, 111
peas, in pods 47
peaches 91
pepper, black 38, 43, 54, 62, 69, 106, 113
peppercorns, black 63, 73, 83, 103
Pimm's No. 1 26
pineapple 113
pine nuts 99
plums 119
pork 73
pork chops 106
potatoes 22, 115
potatoes, new 65

raisins 109
redcurrants 71
rhubarb 18
rice, long-grain brown 99
rosemary 60, 73

saffron 111
sage leaves 51, 63, 83, 106
salad burnet 65
salmon, fresh fillets 38
savory 67
sea salt 54, 62, 63, 69, 73, 83, 85, 103, 106, 109, 115

sesame paste 43
sherry, medium 28
sherry, sweet 85, 119
sorrel leaves 69
spring onions 65
stock 51, 60, 69, 83, 99
strawberries 26
suet, beef 109
sugar 115
sugar, Barbados 93, 96, 101
sugar, Demerara 16, 91, 119
sultanas 101, 109
sunflower oil 32, 34, 69, 78
sweet cicely 71

tahini 43
tansy 73
tarragon 76
thyme 51, 78
tomatoes 20, 43
tomato puree 36
tonic water 26
trout 89
turmeric 99, 117

vanilla pod 18, 119
vermouth, dry 26
vinegar, red wine 60
vinegar, white wine 91

white wine 38
whiting 40
woodruff 81

yeast 85, 93, 115
yoghurt, natural 47, 54, 81, 99, 113

zucchini 49

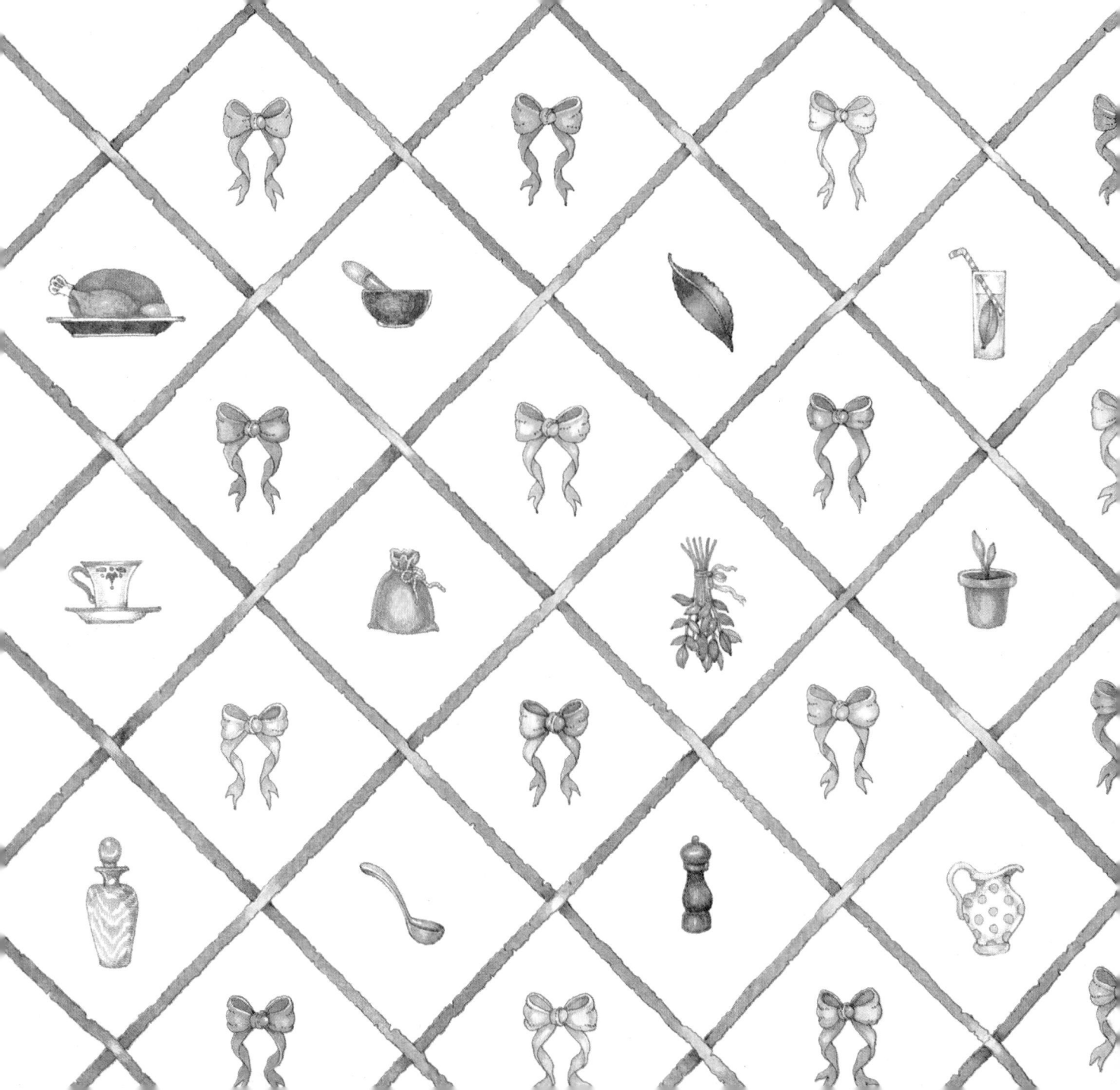